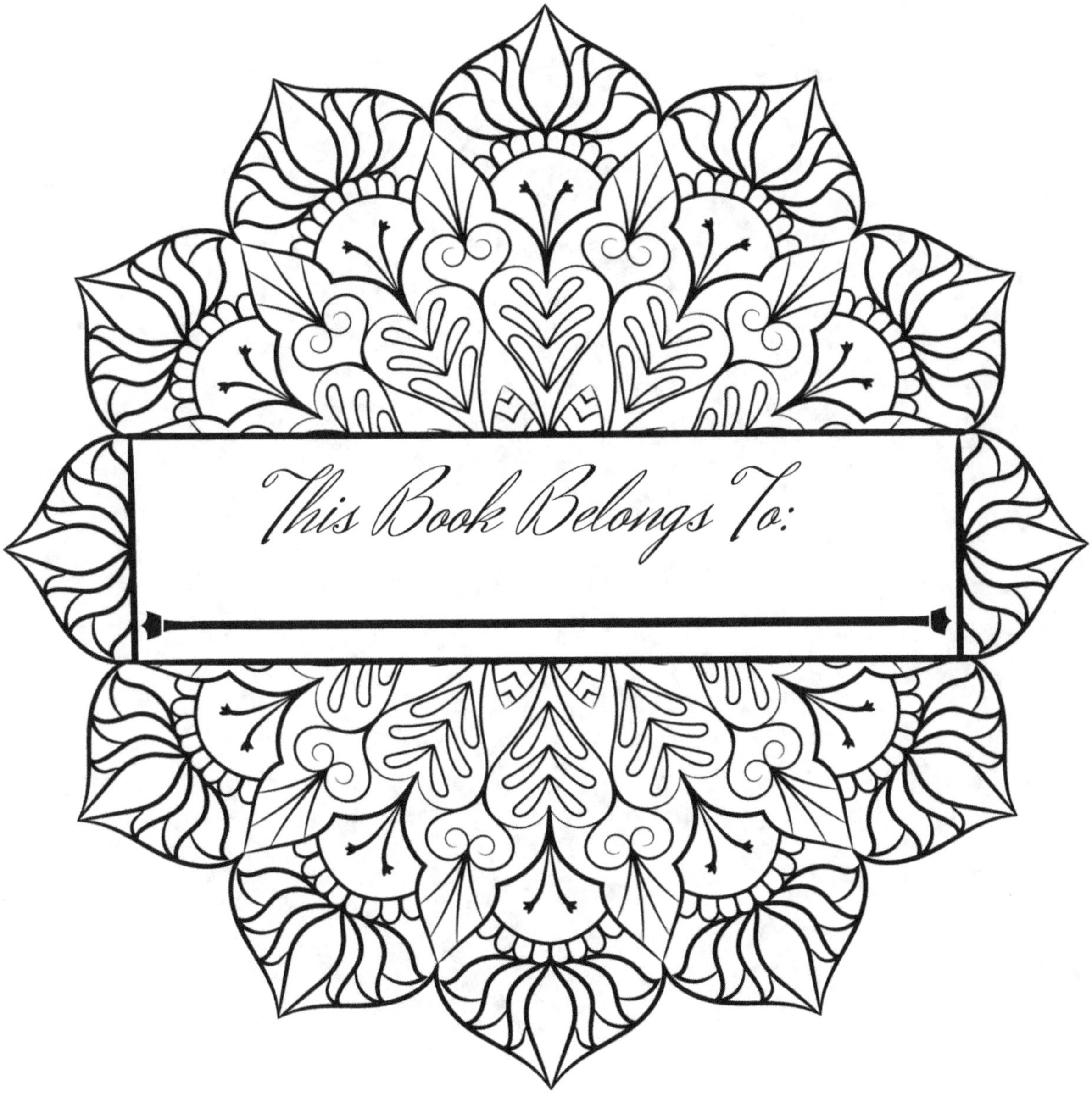
This Book Belongs To:

Mandala Dreams

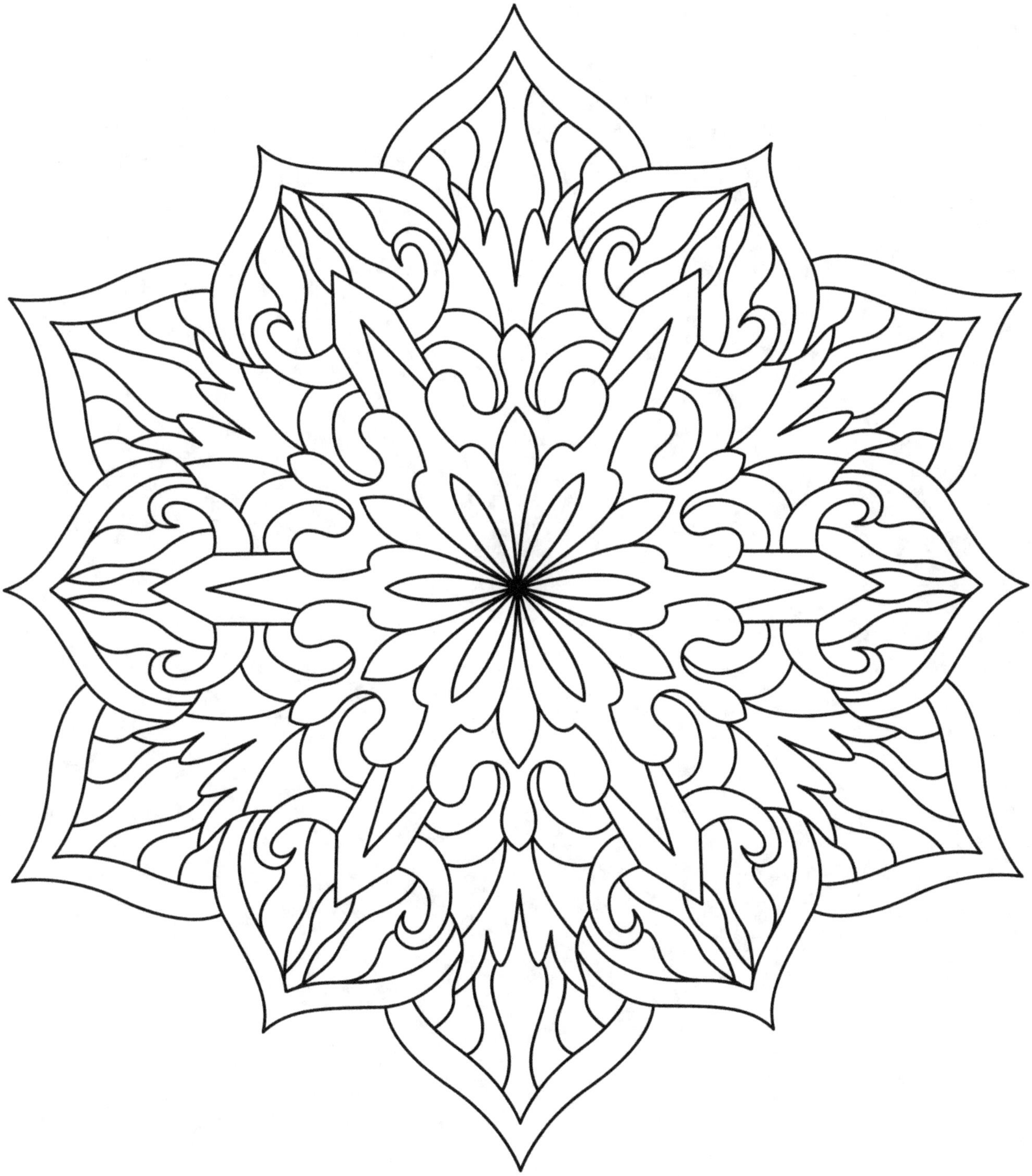

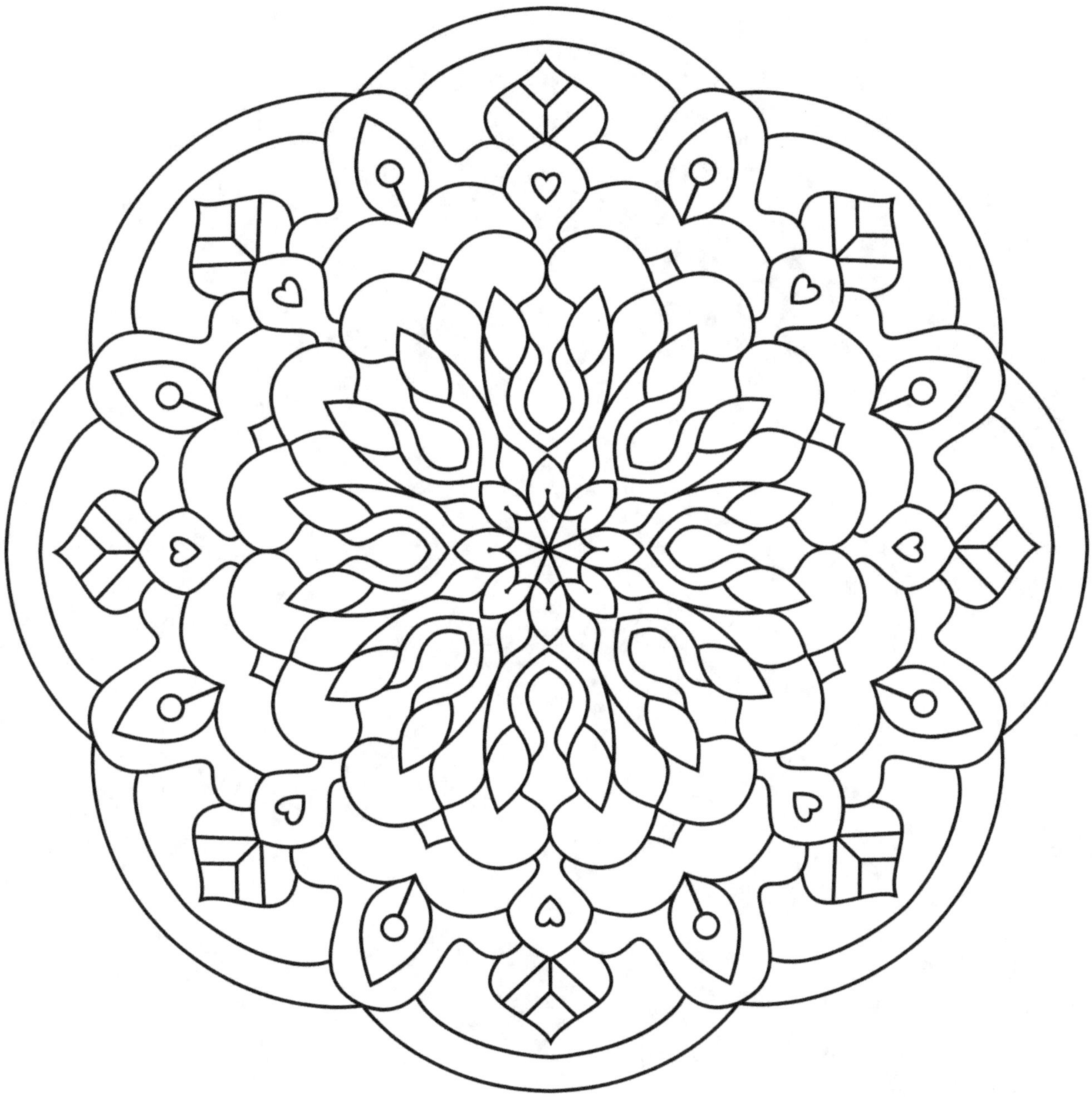

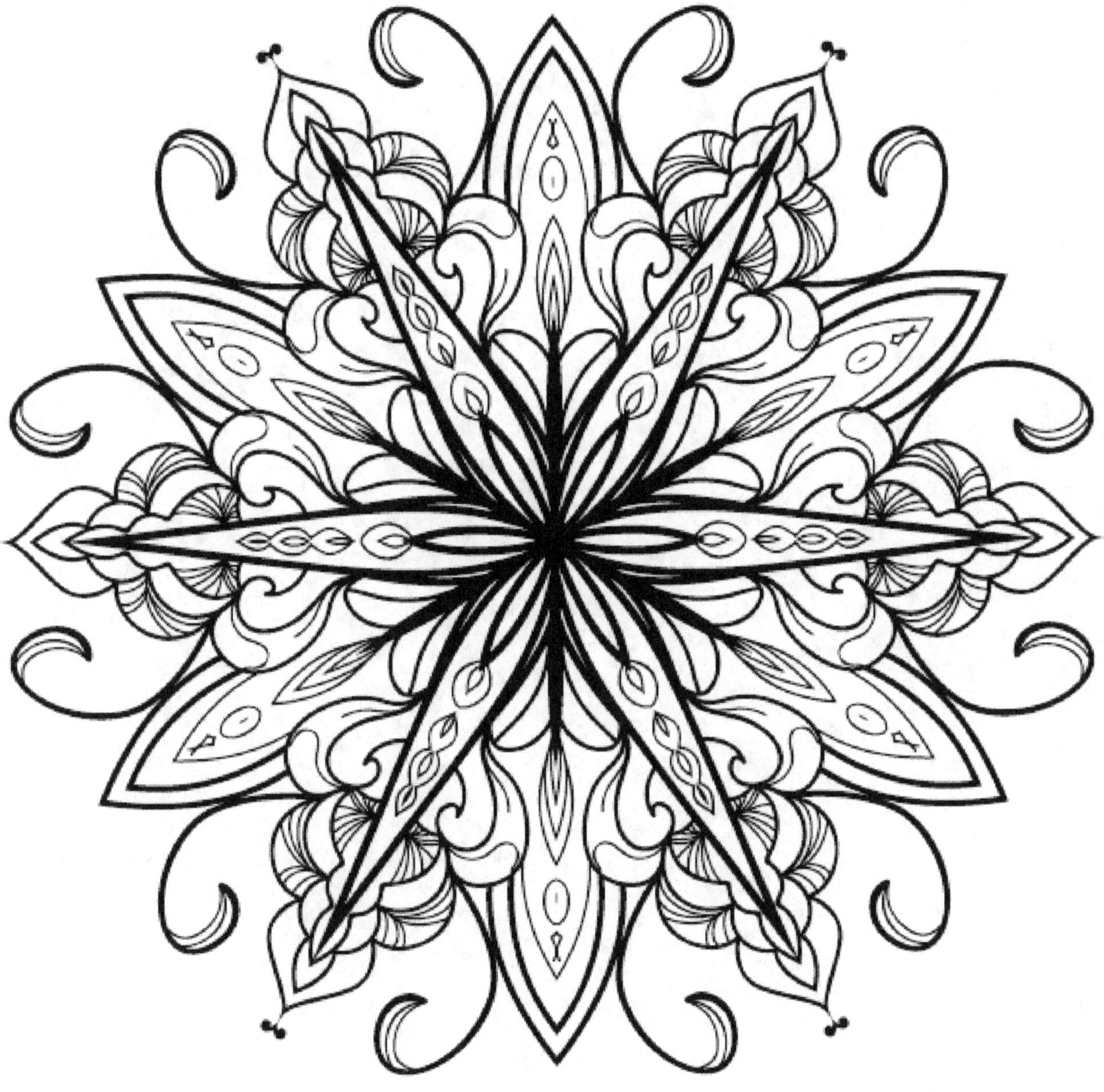

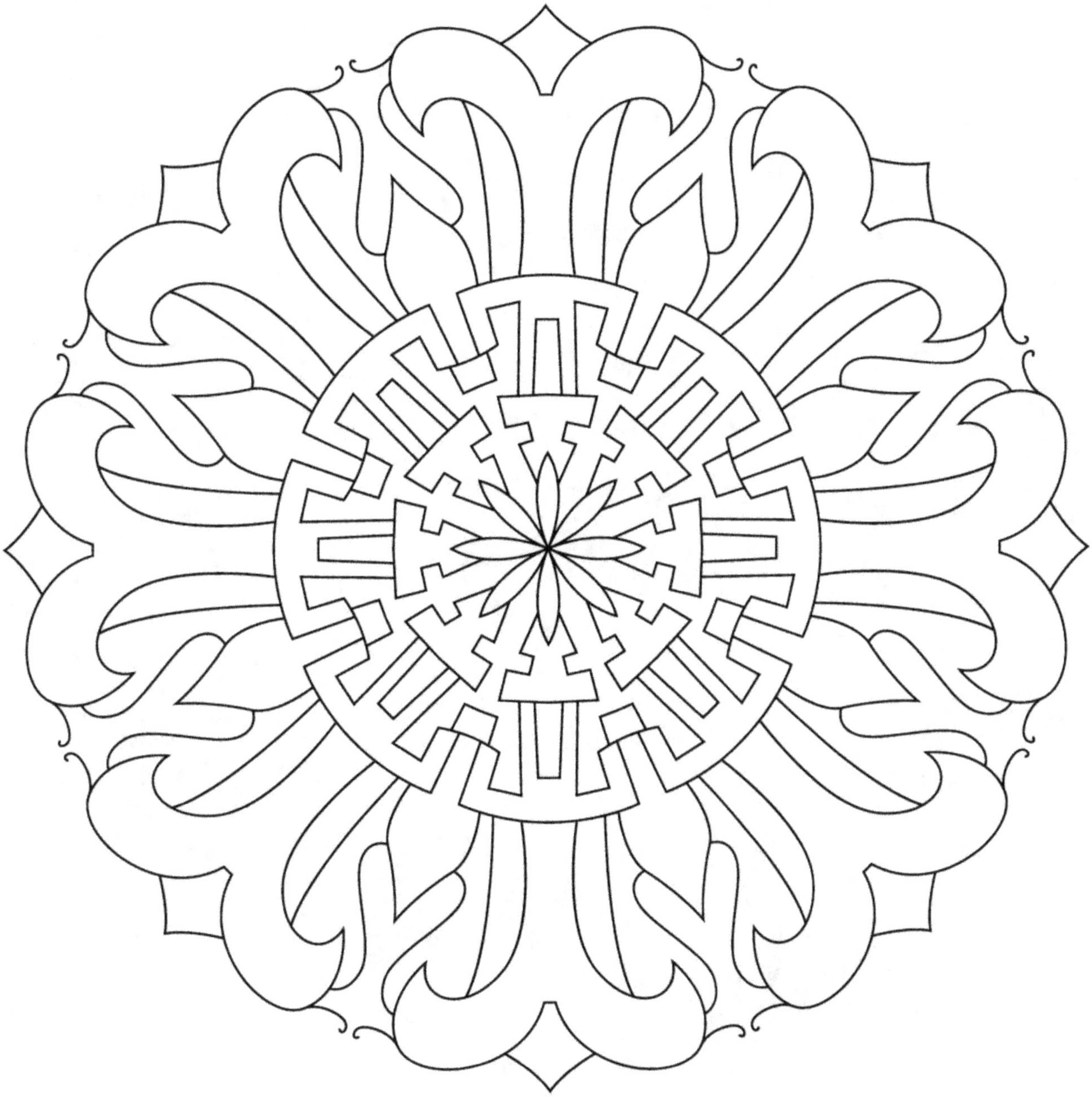

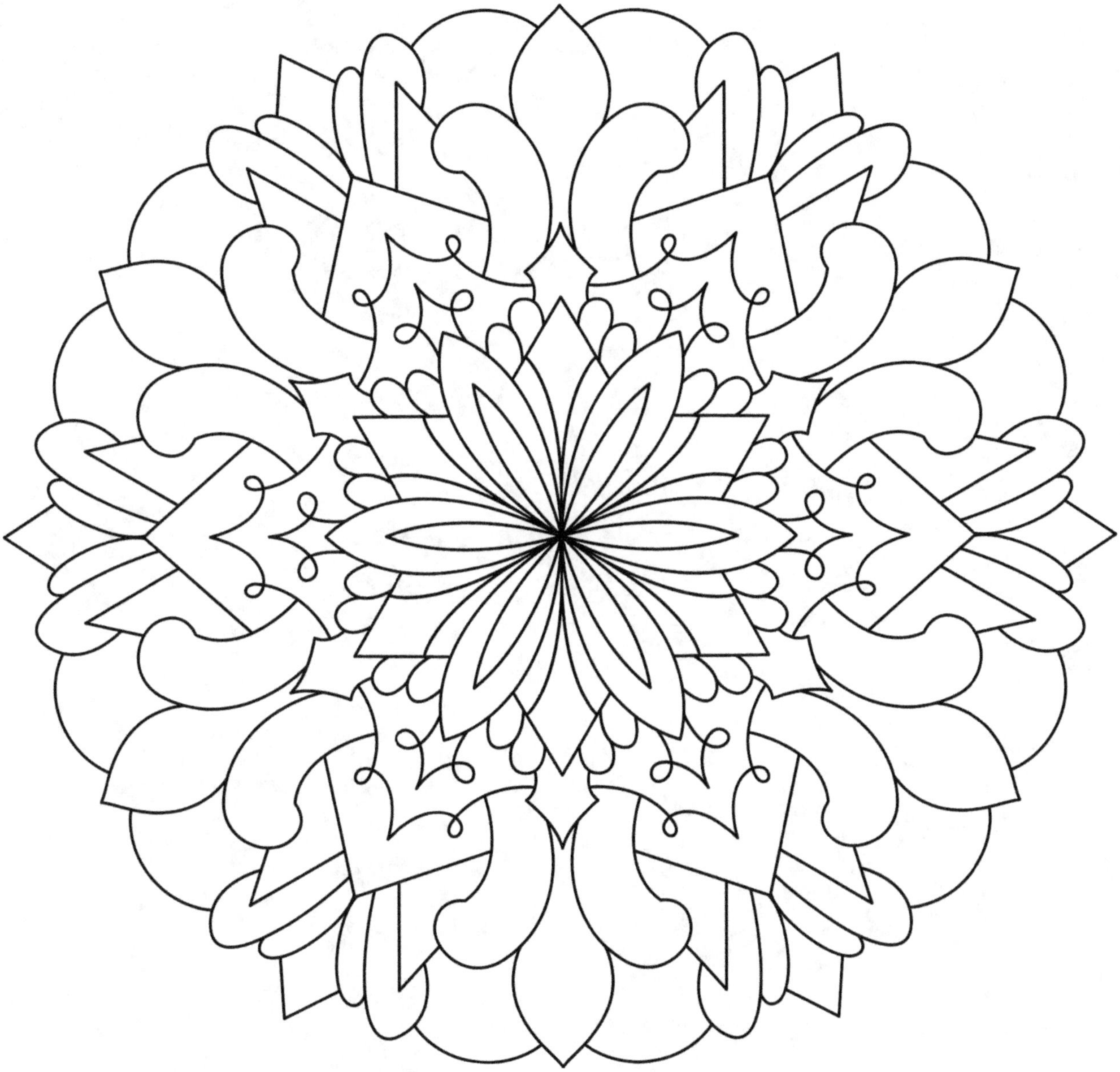

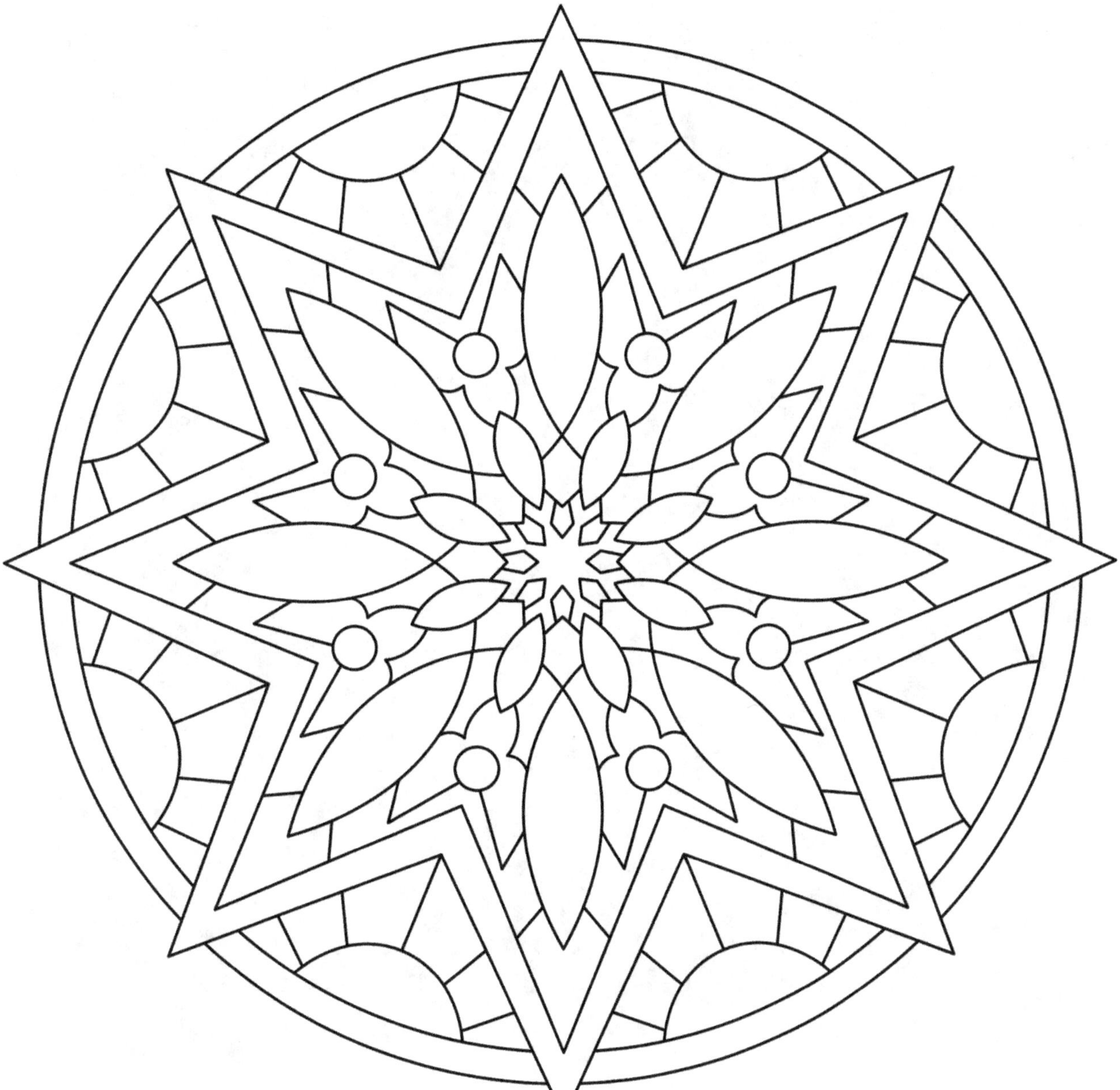

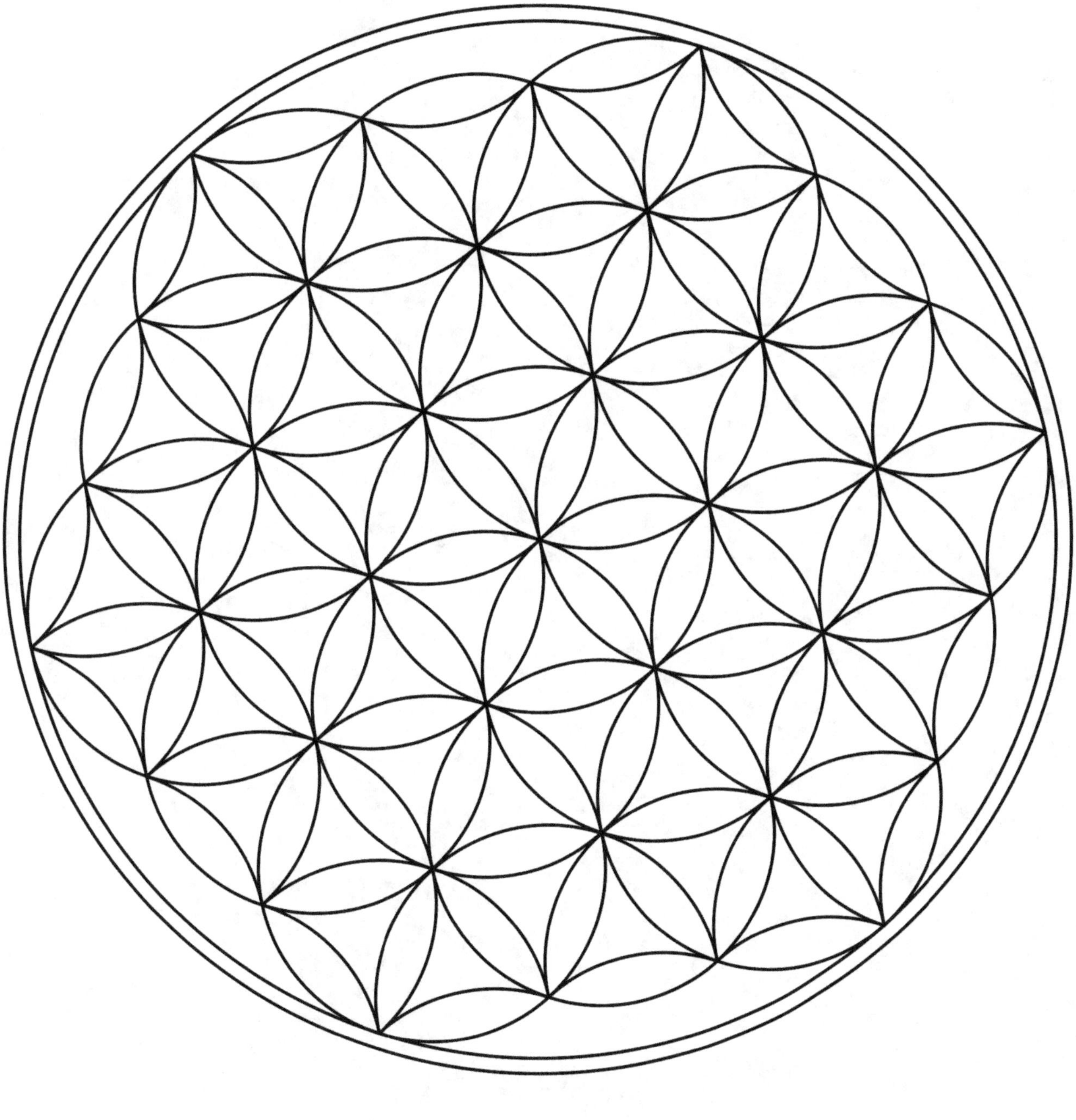

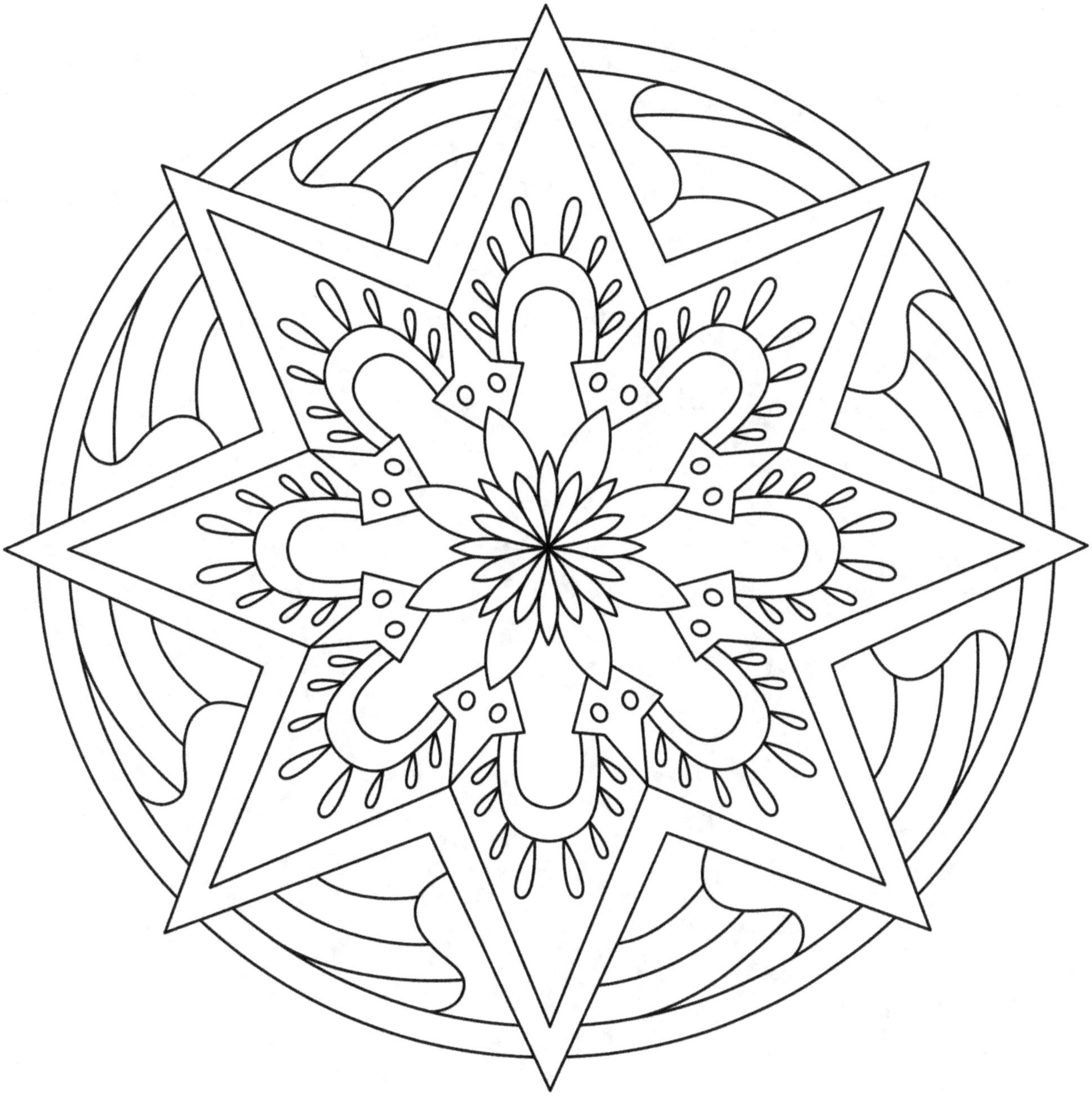

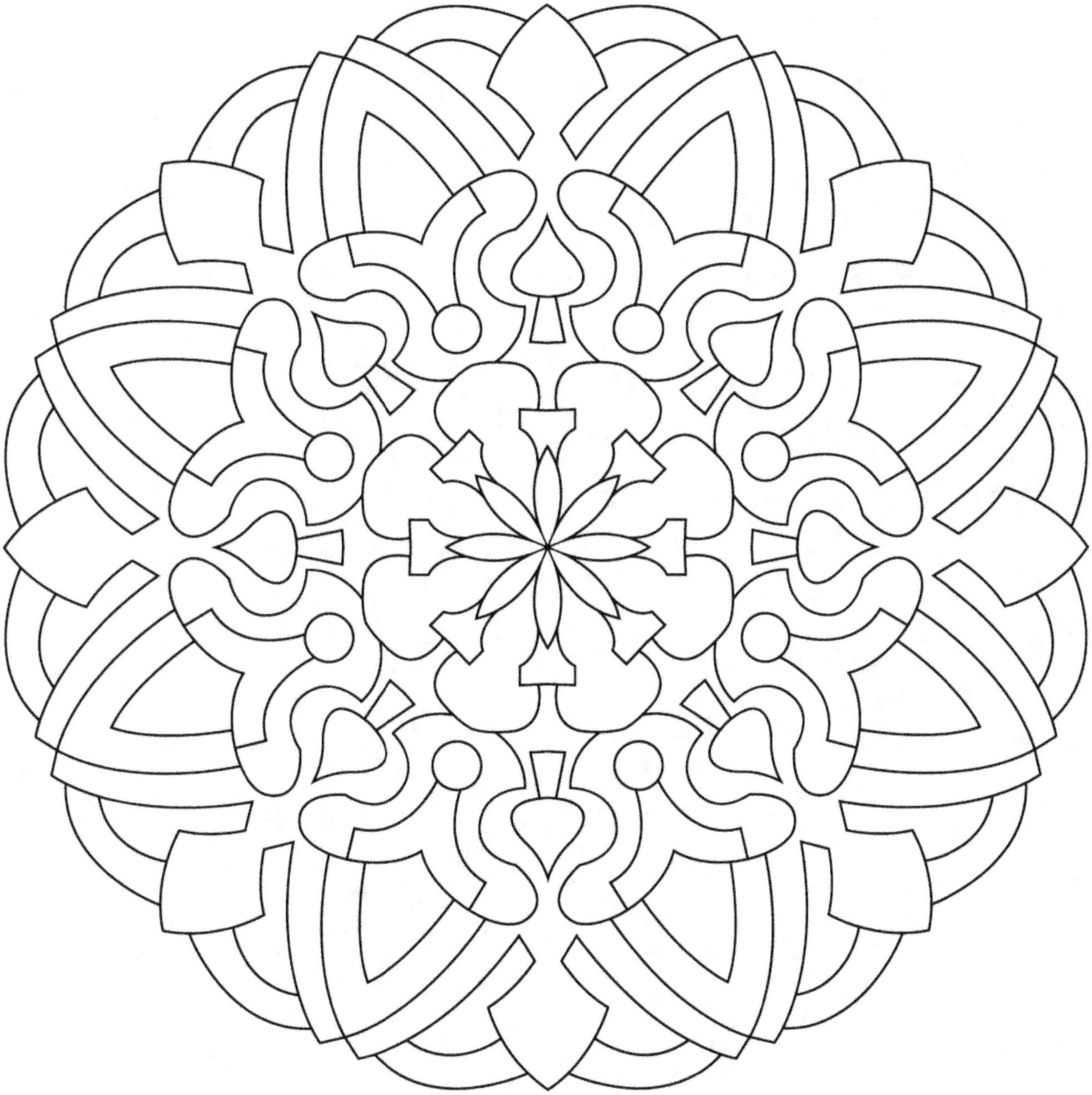

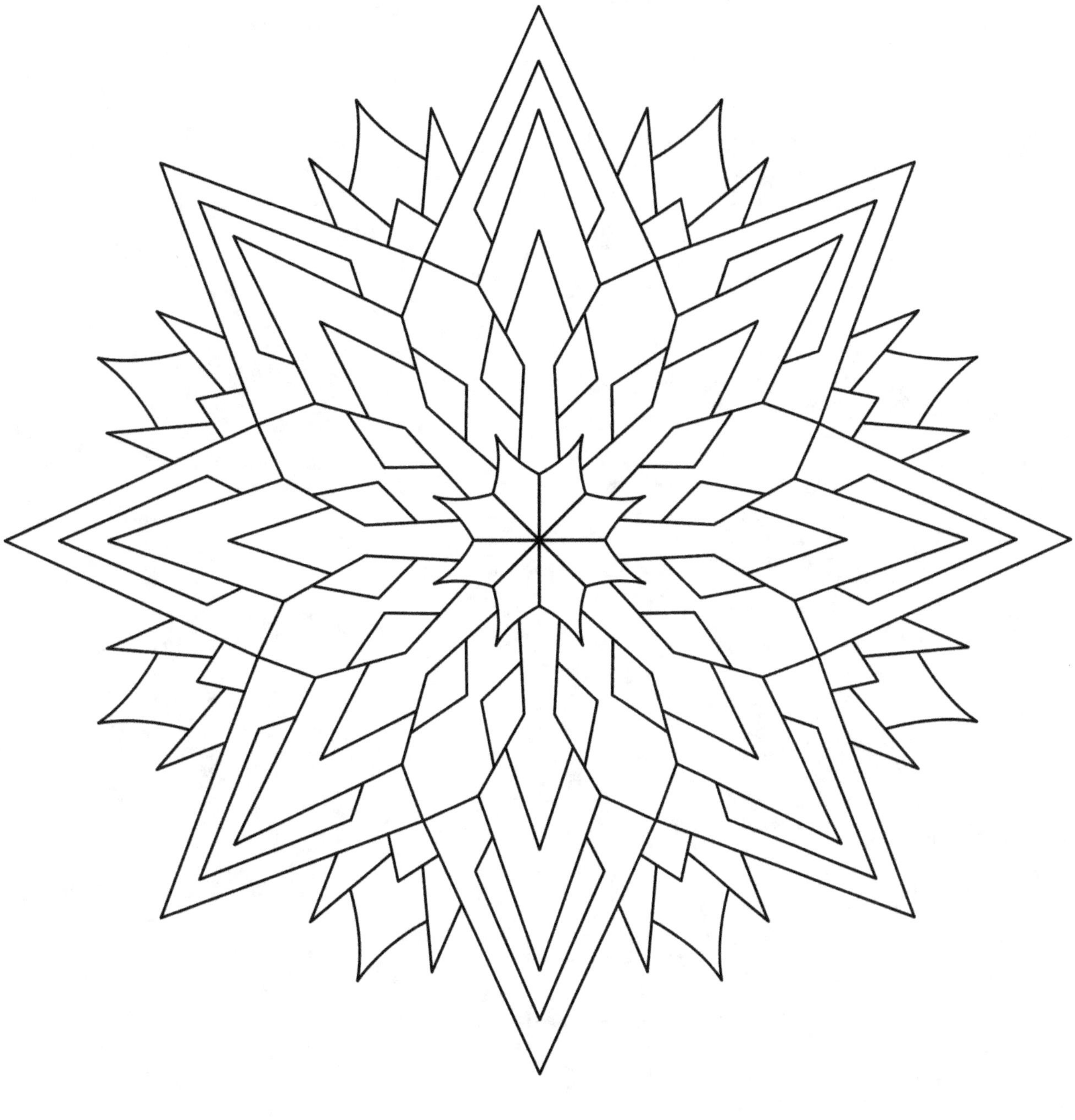

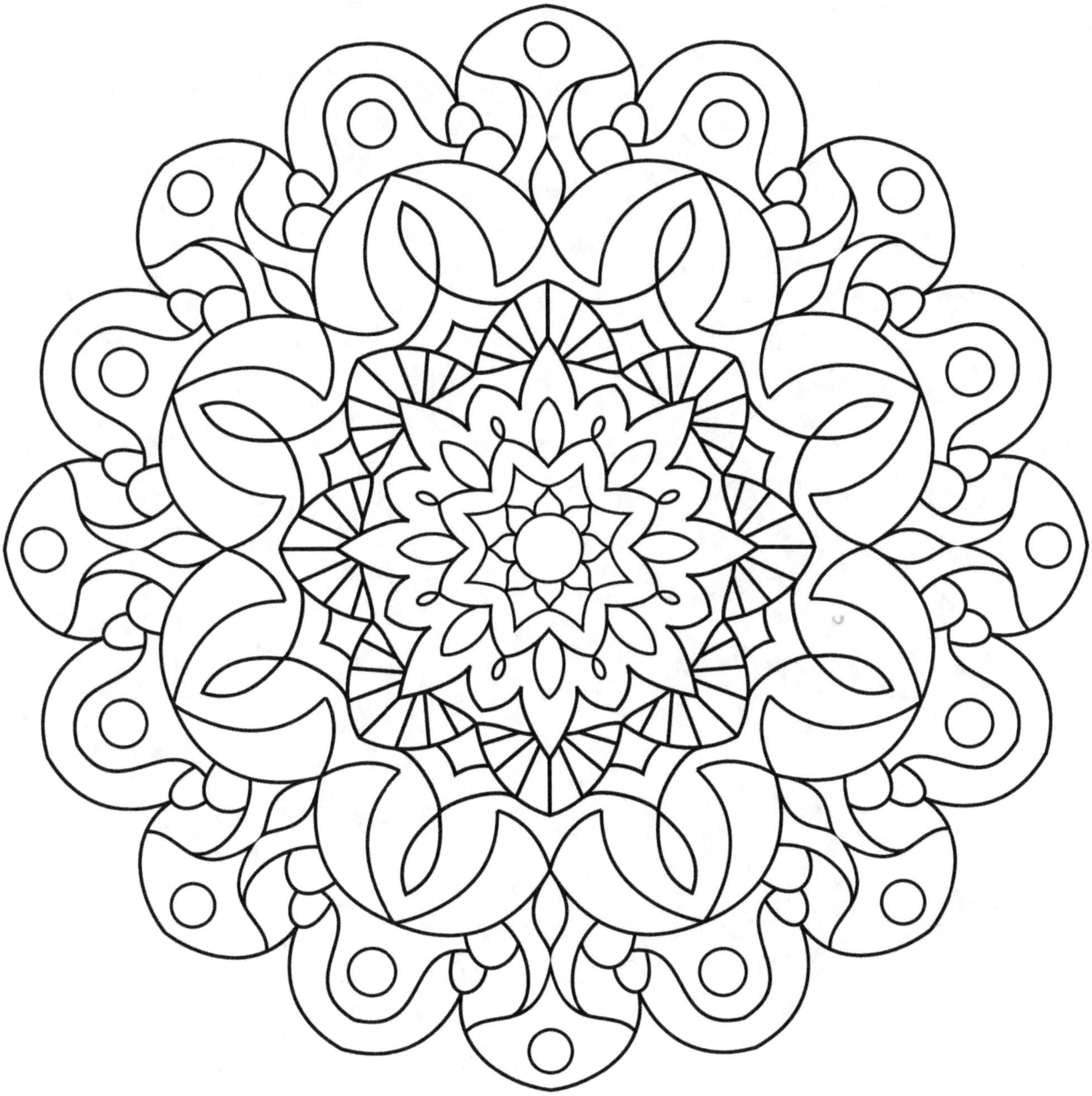

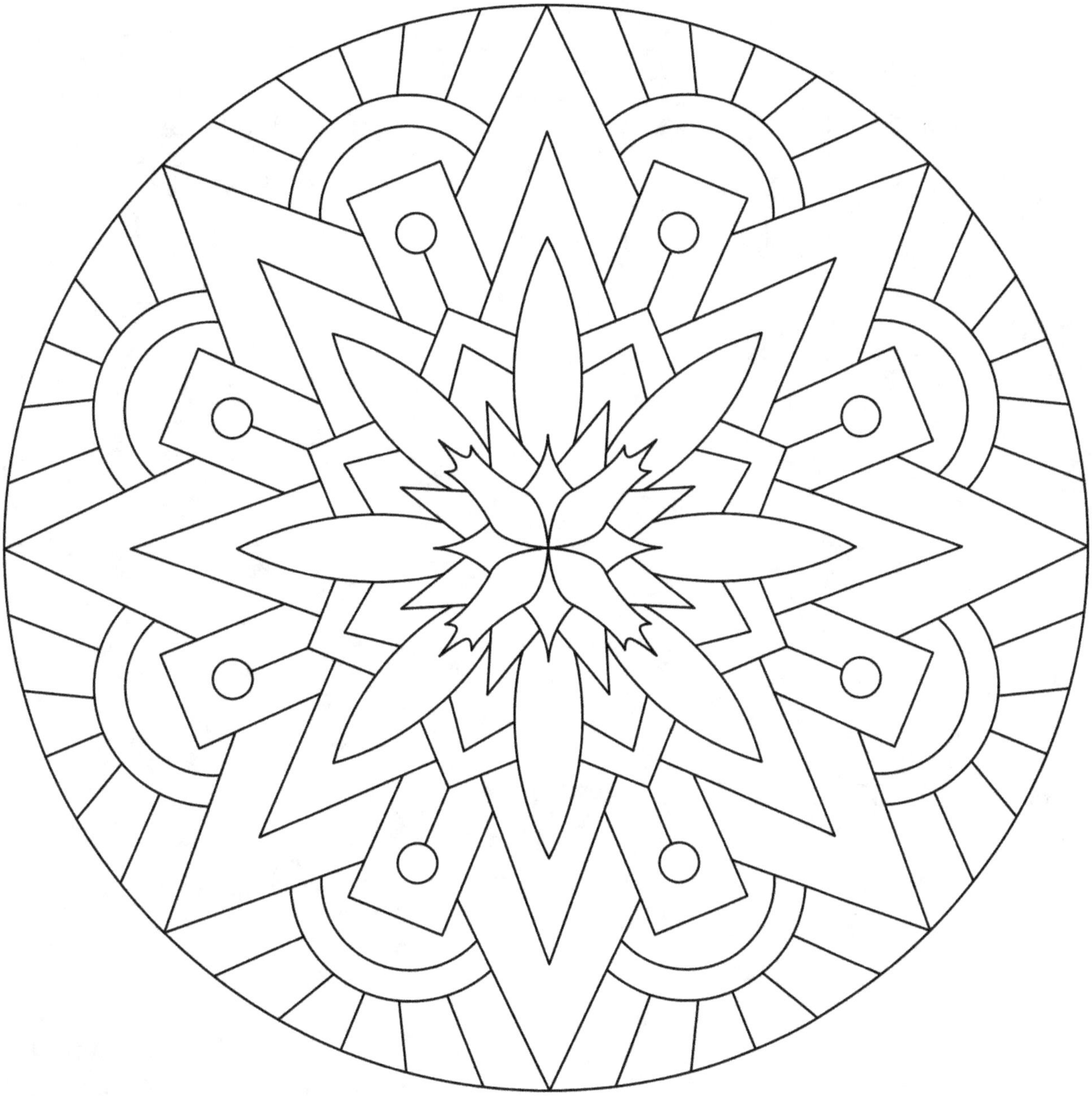

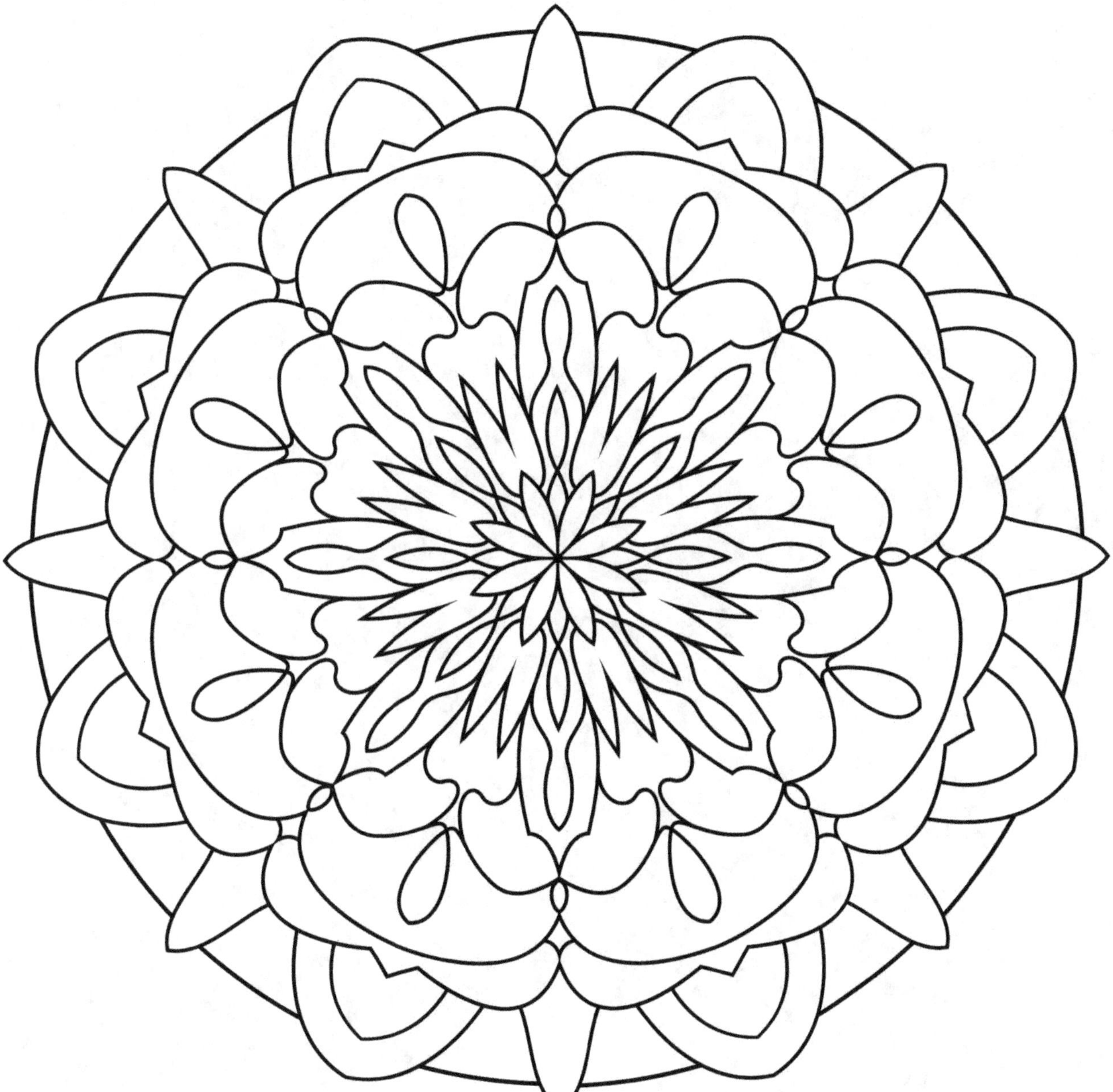

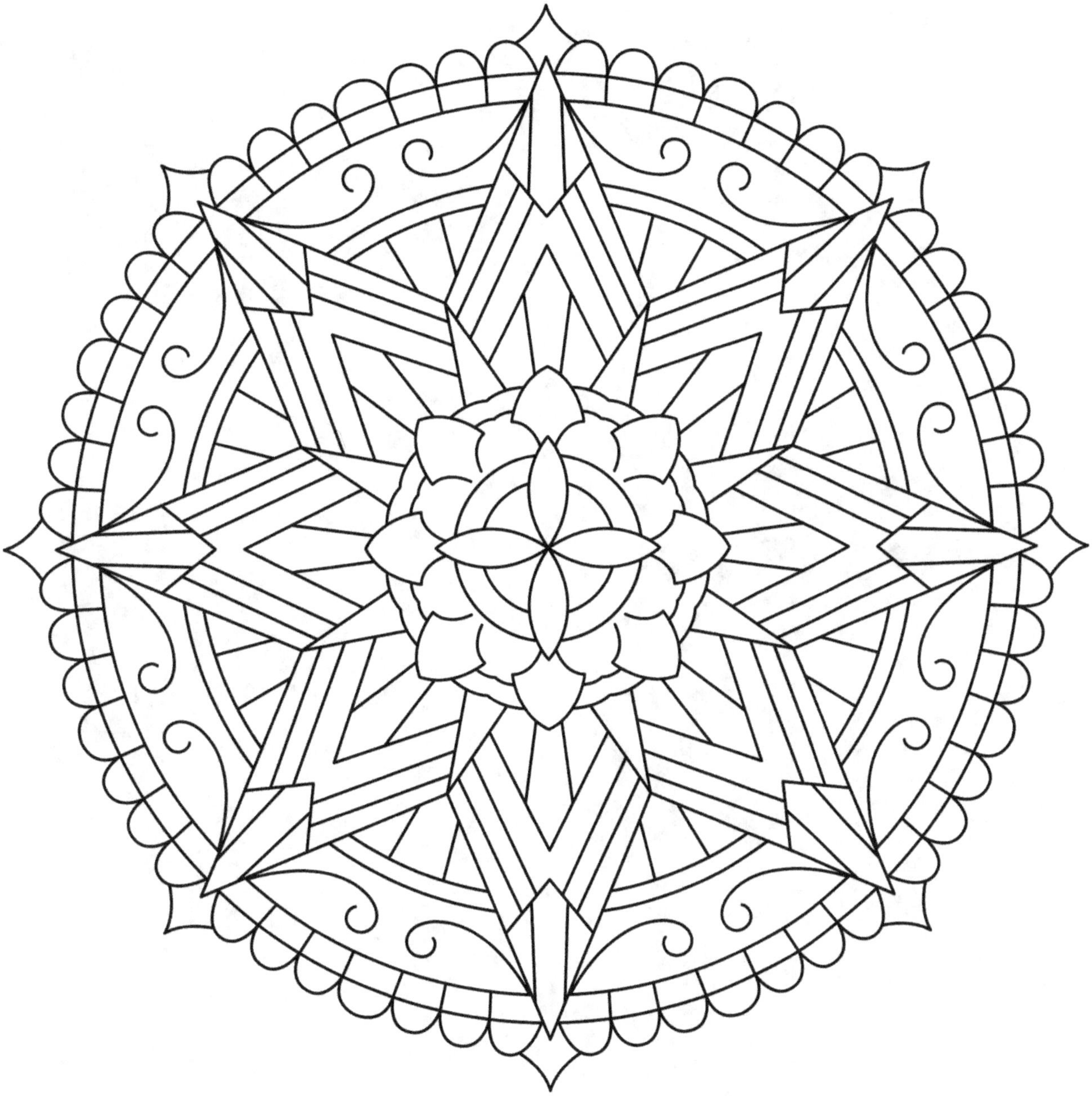

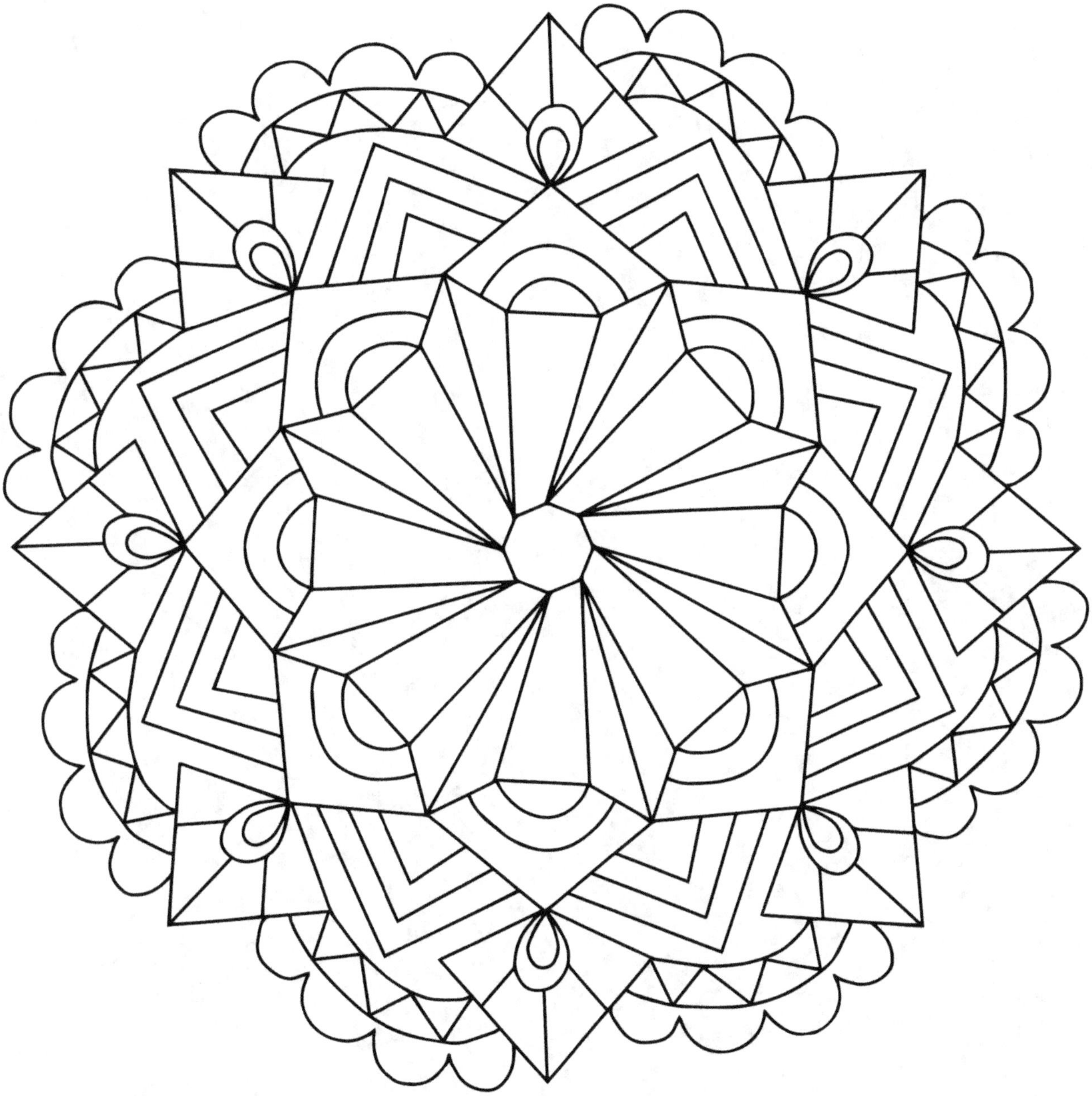

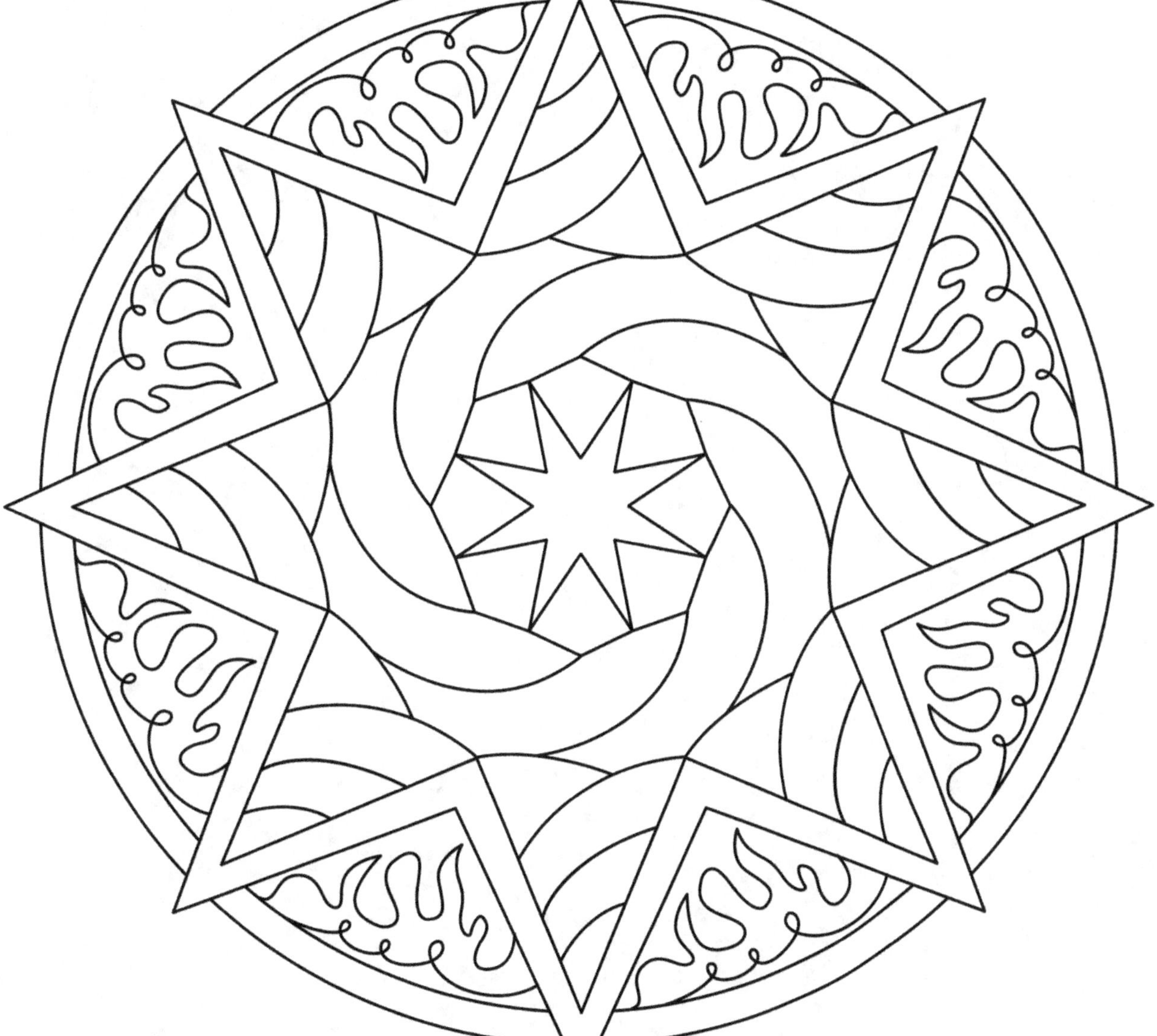

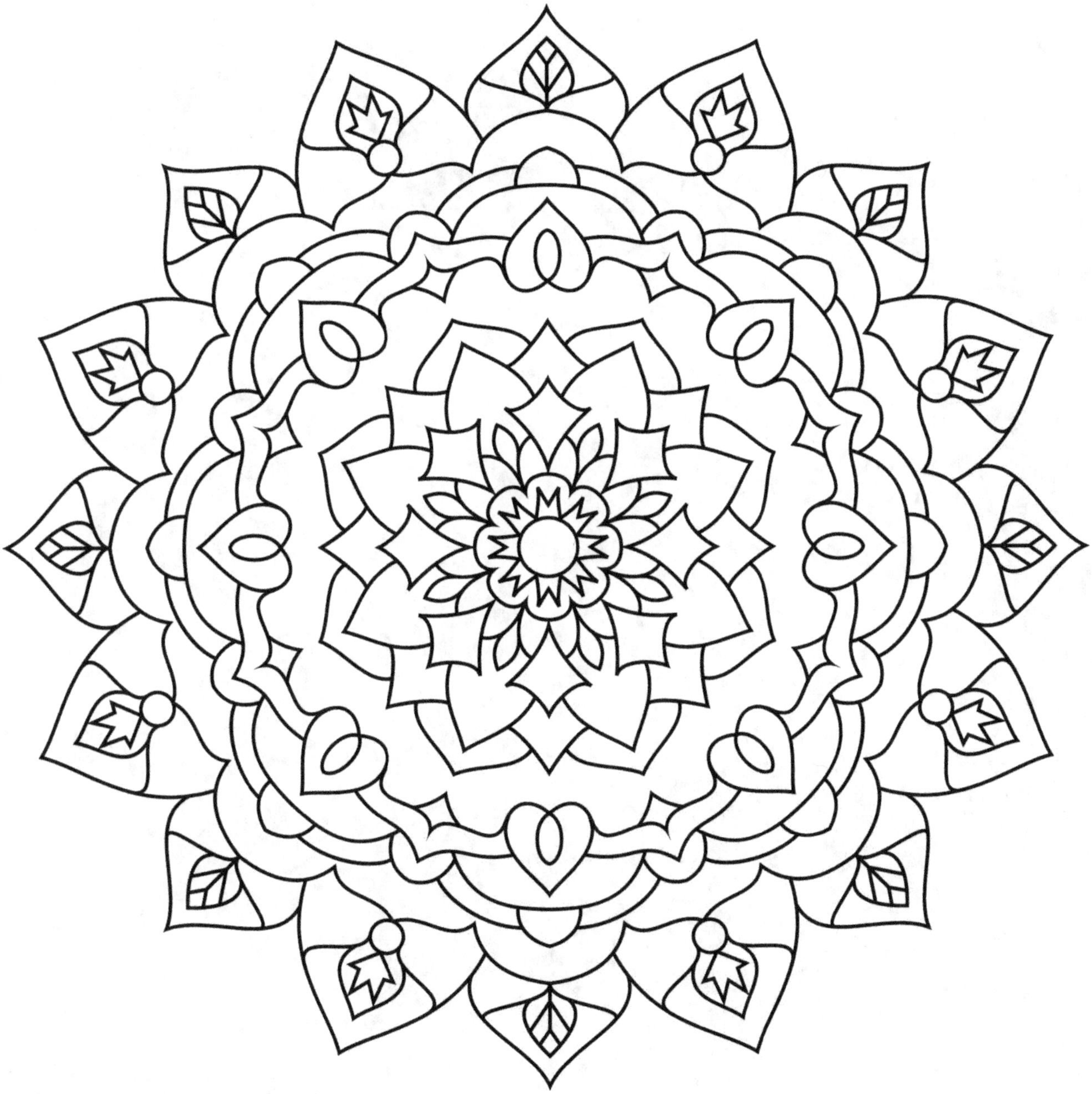

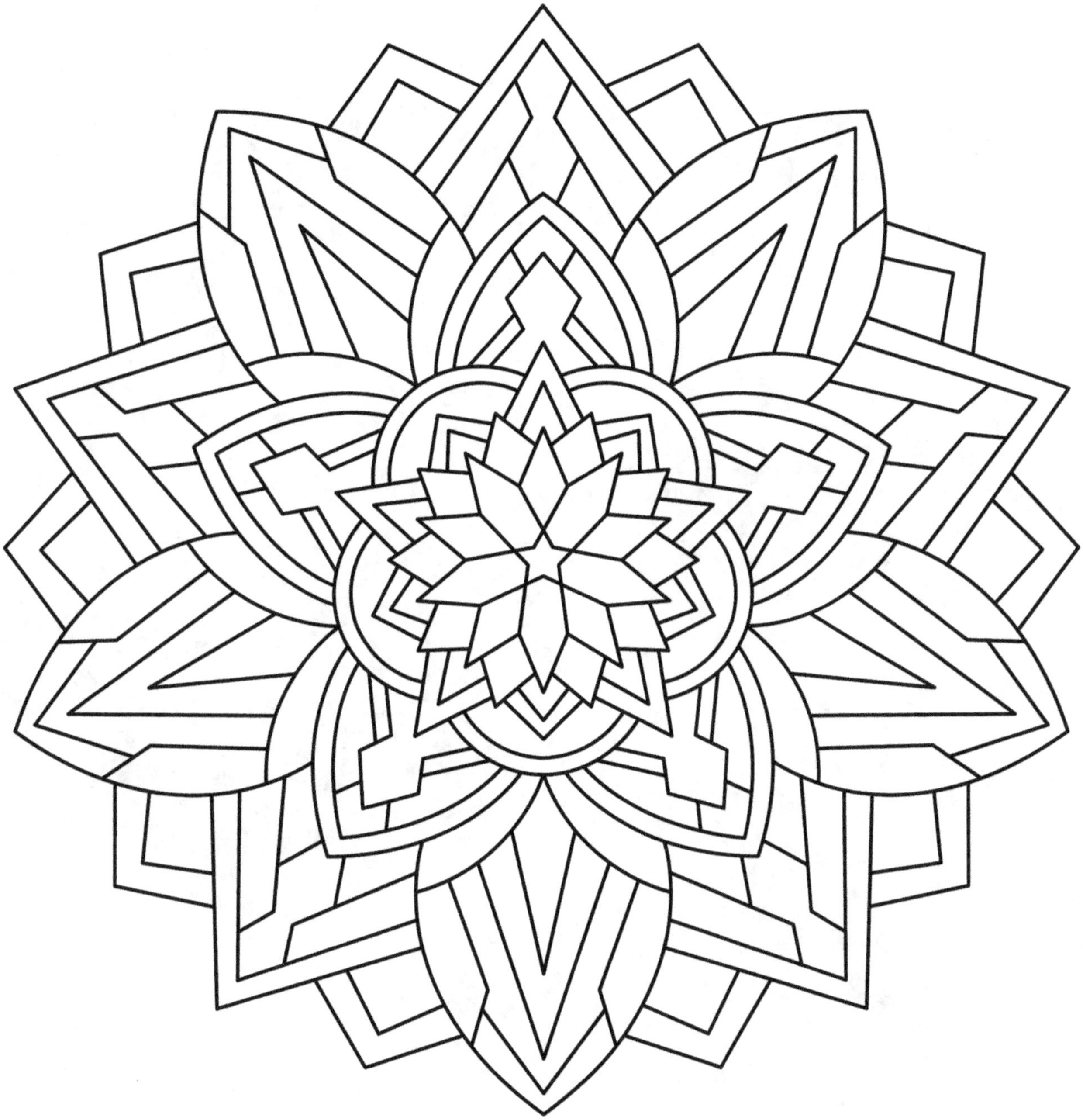

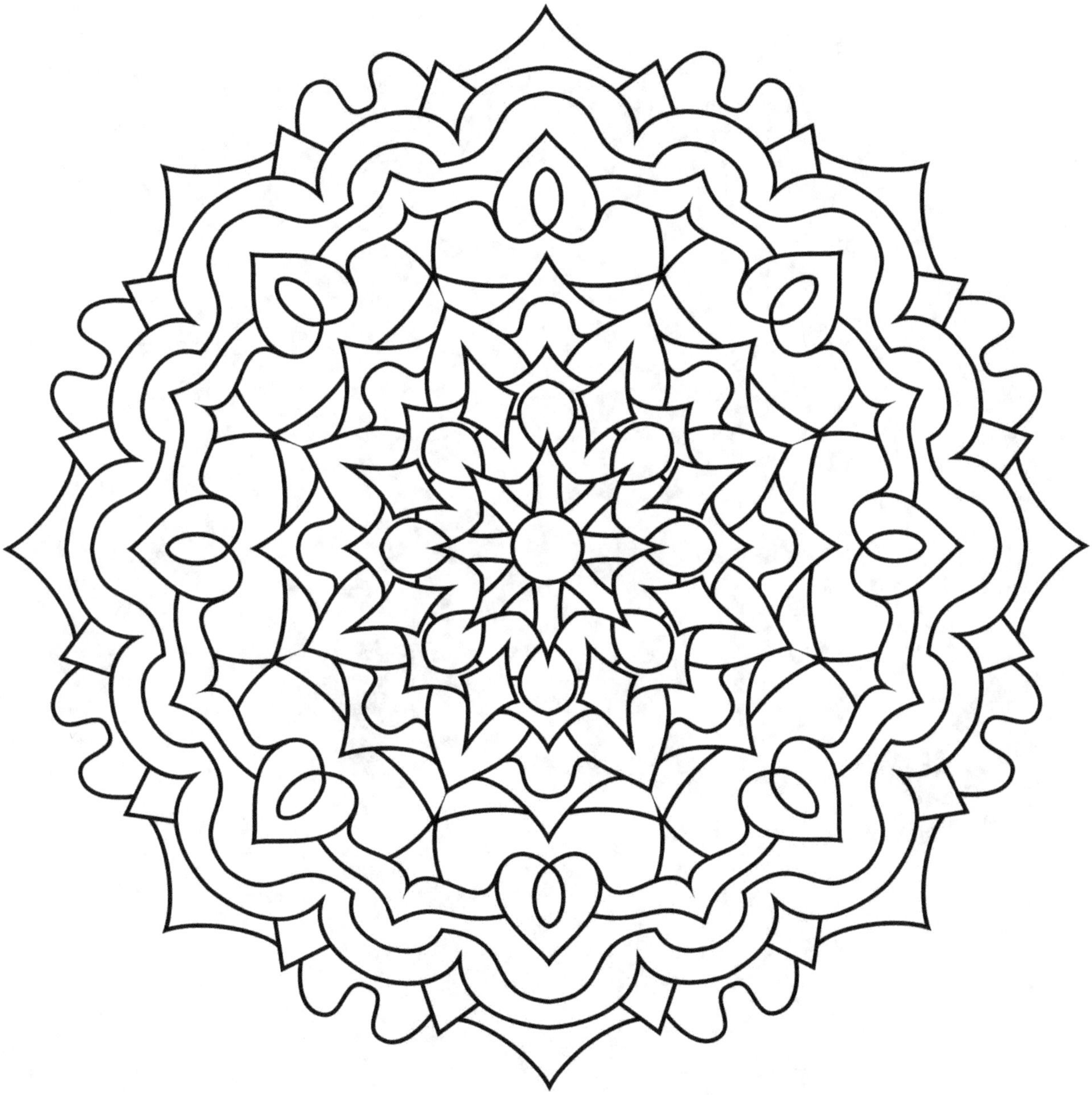

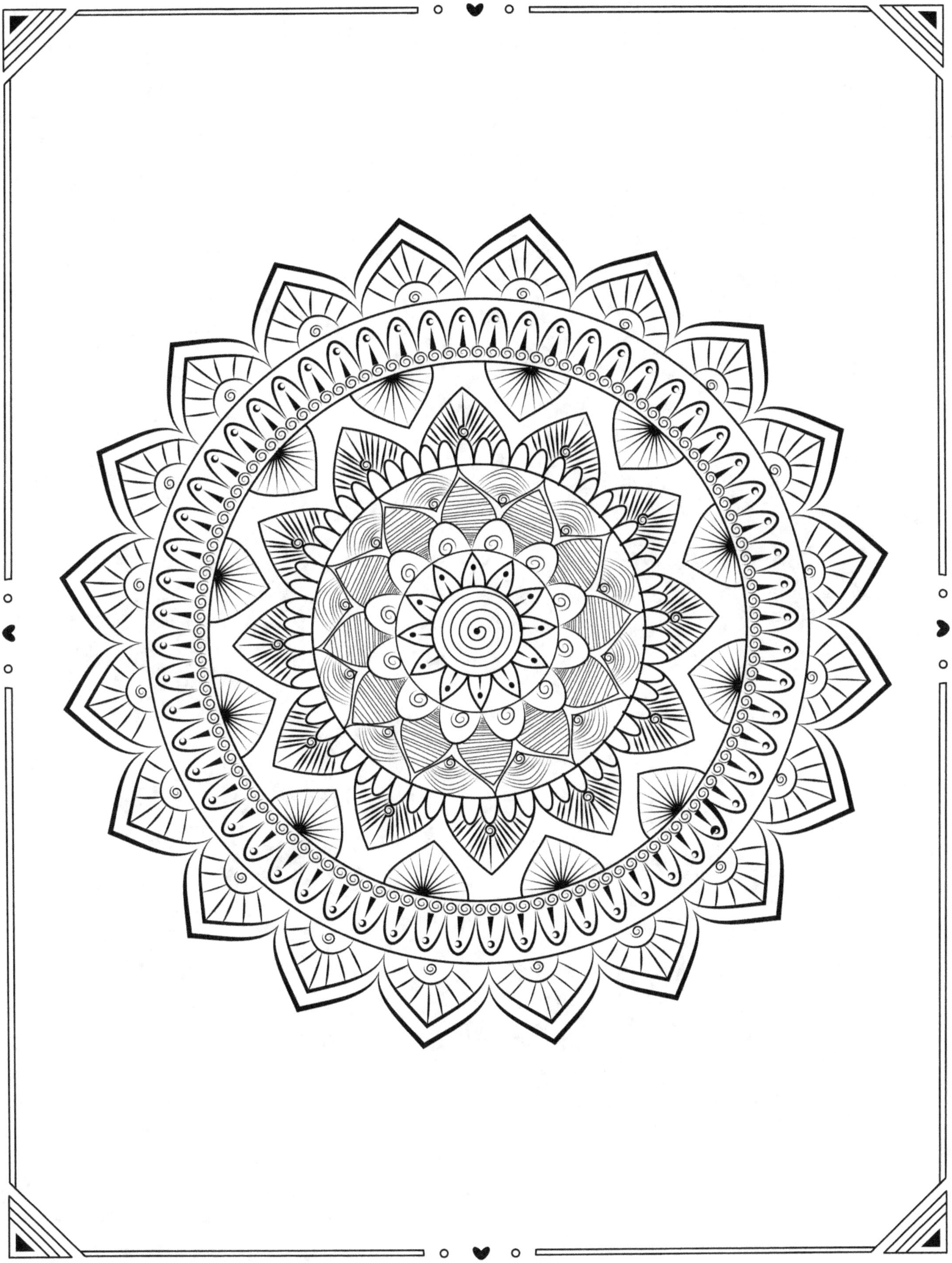

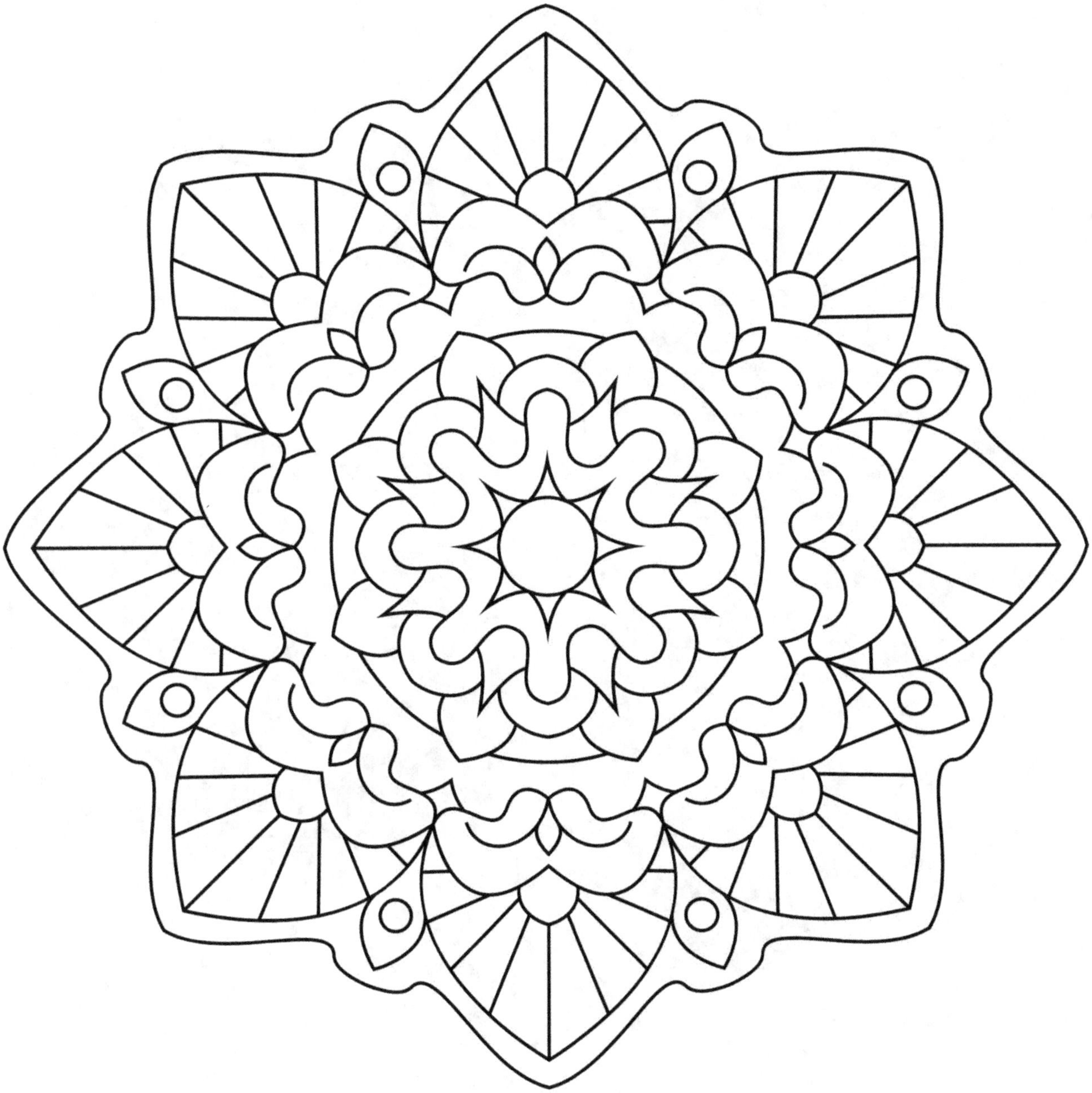

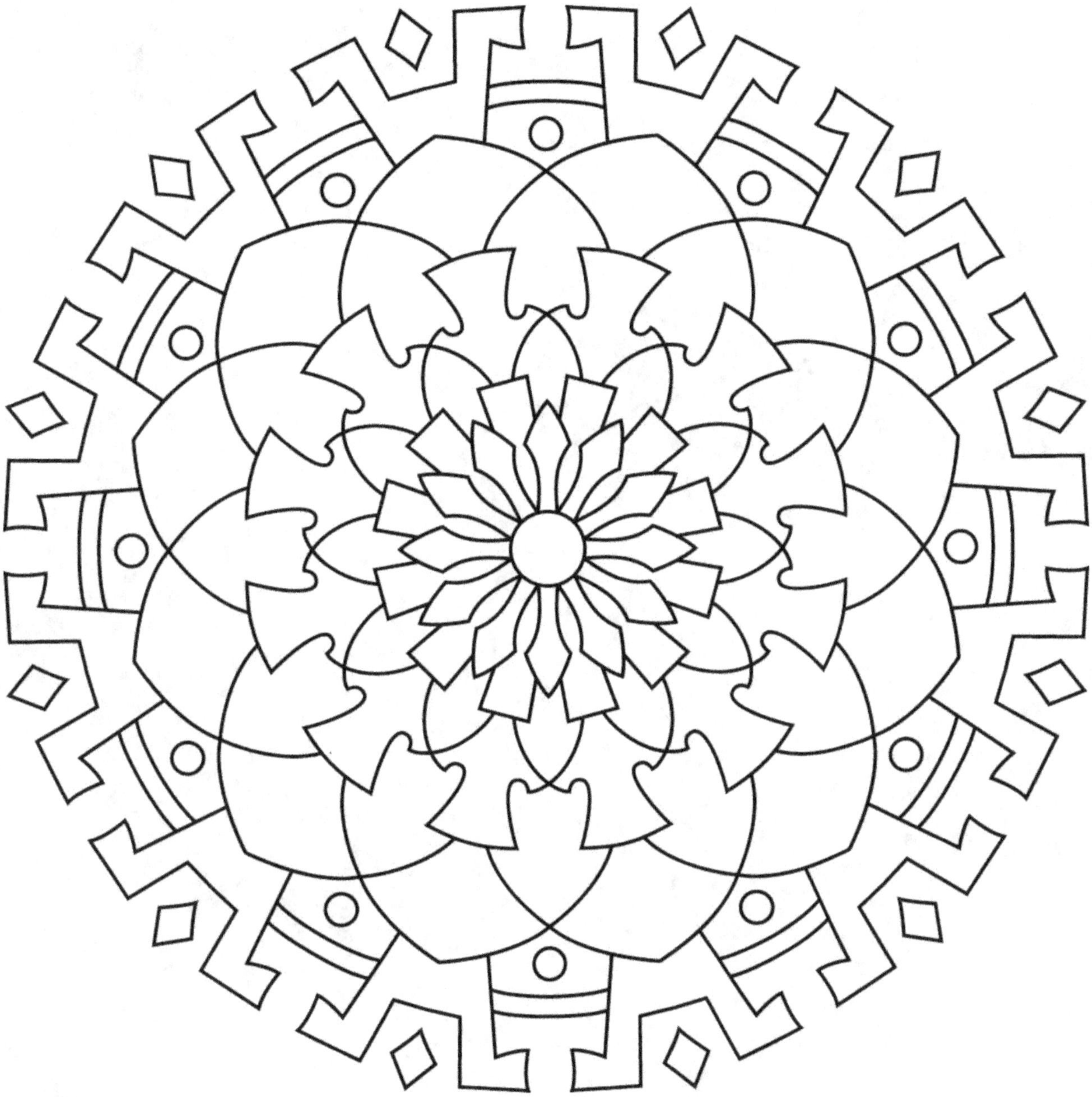

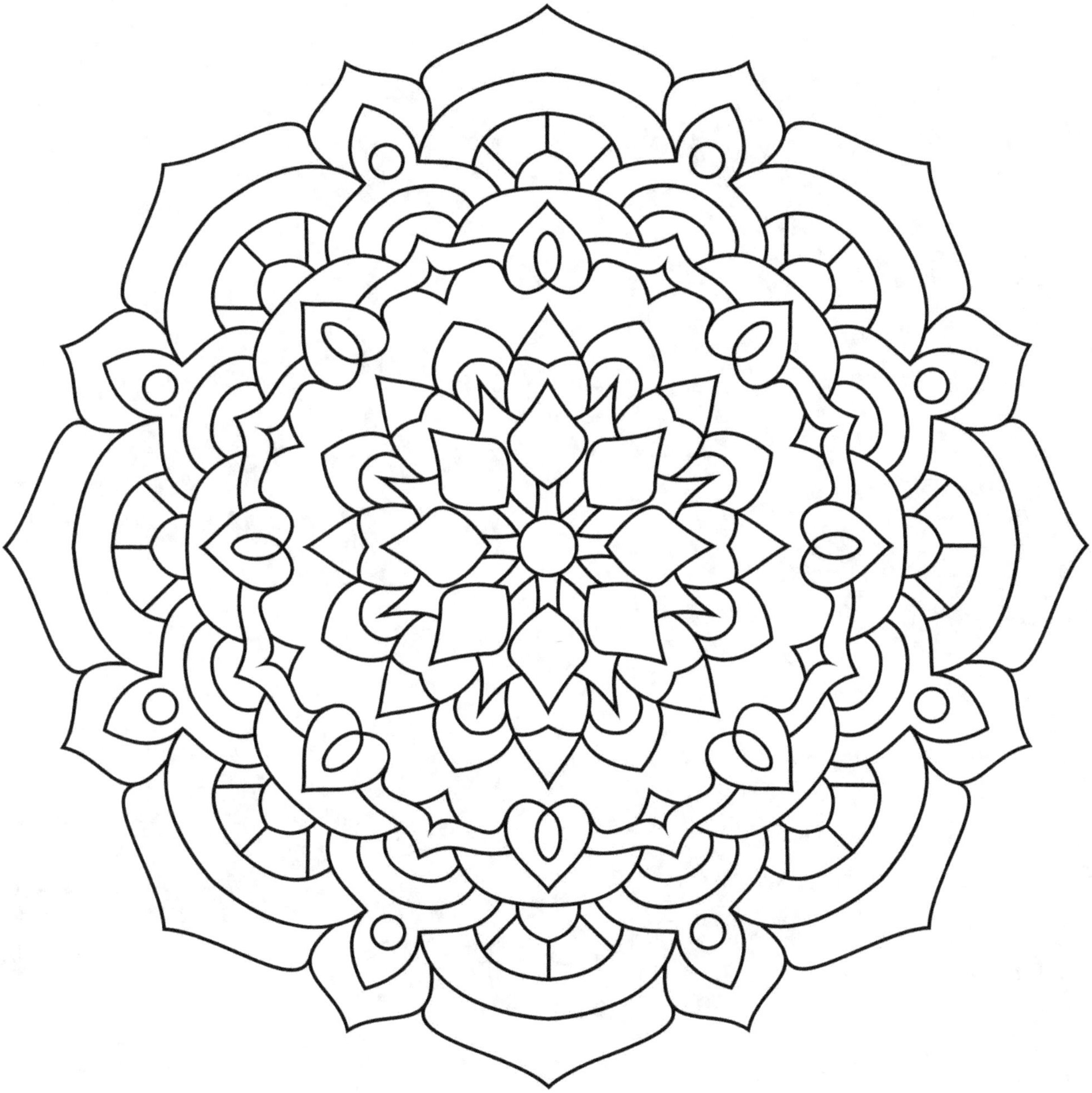

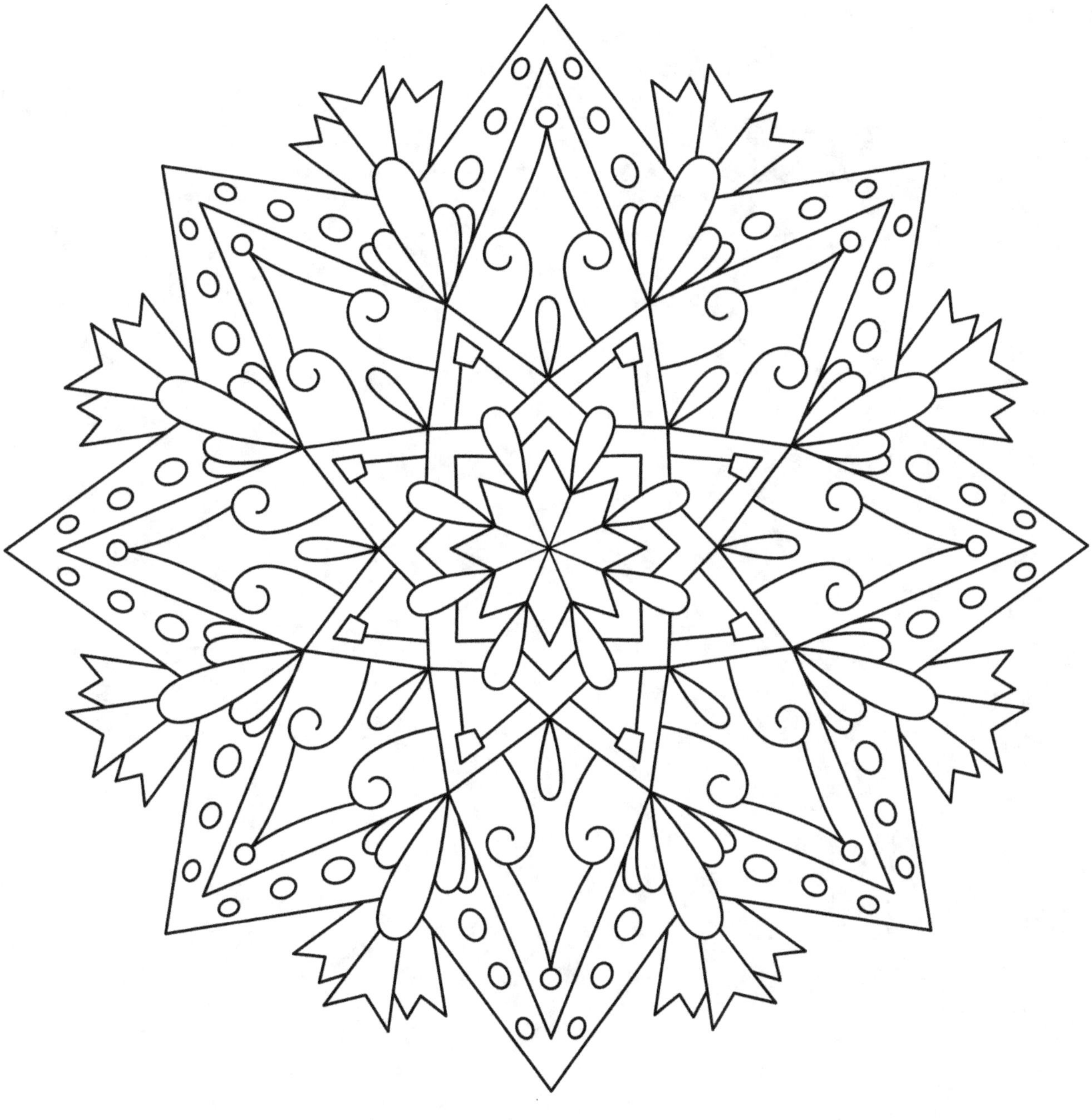

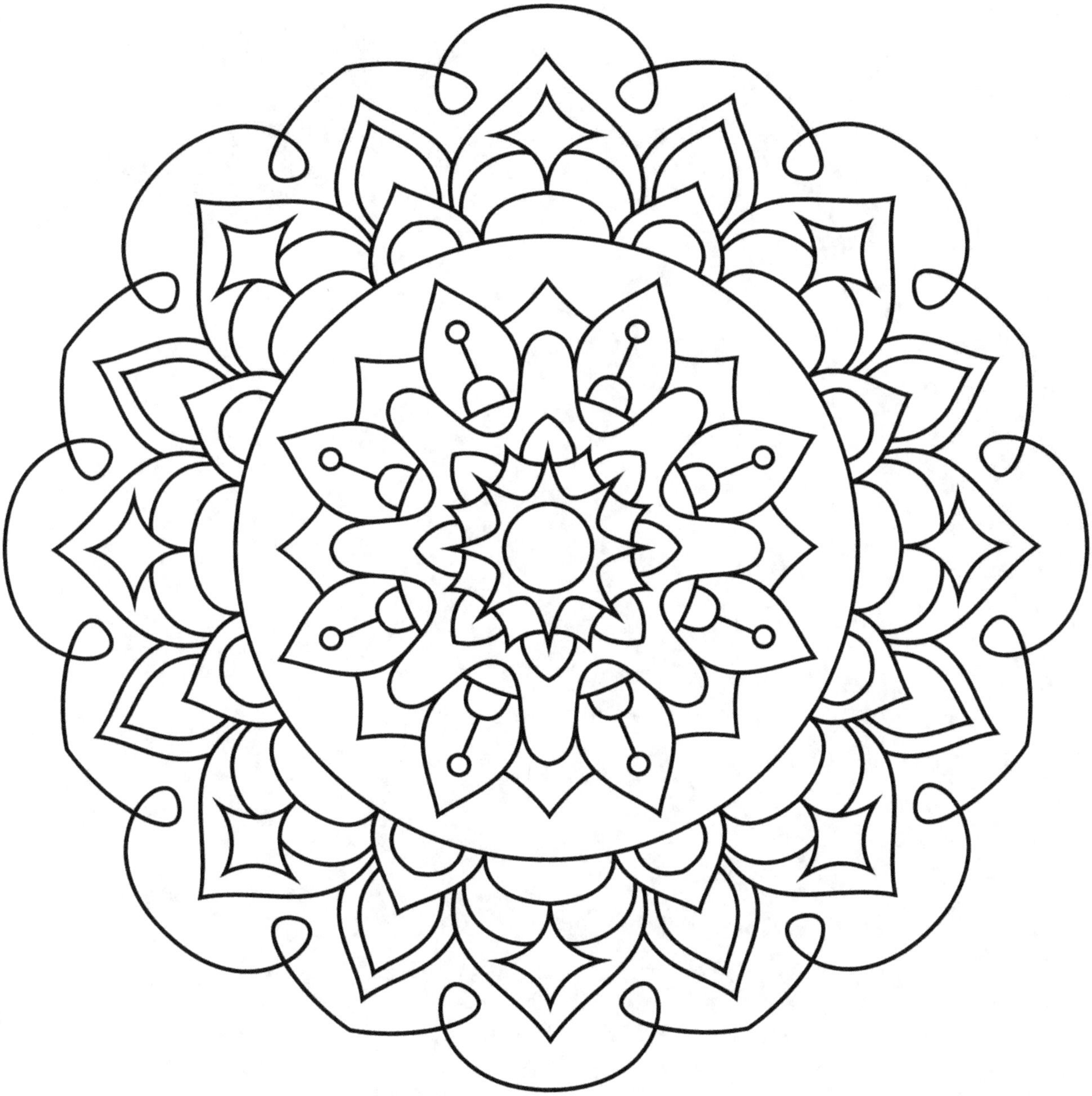

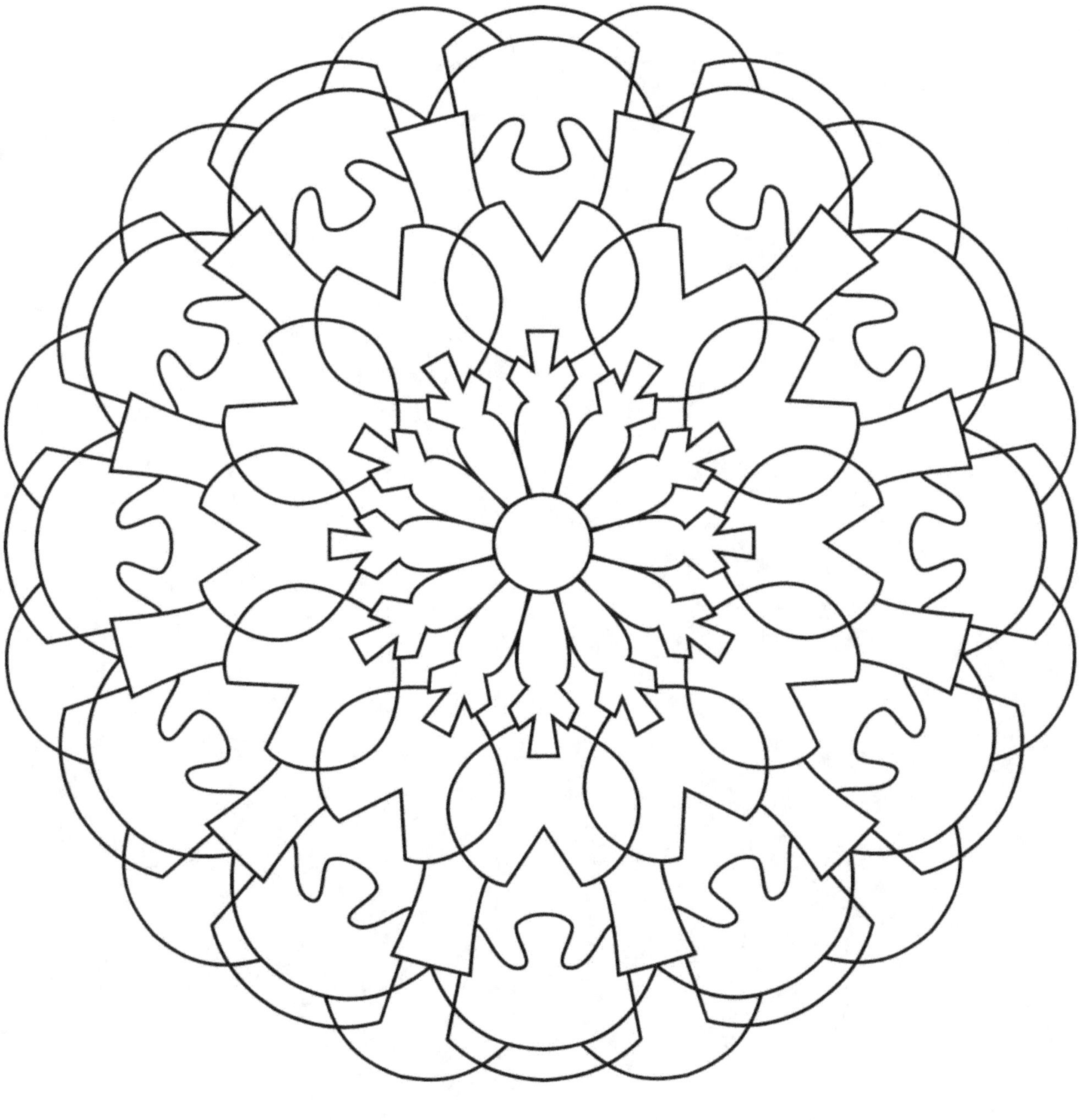

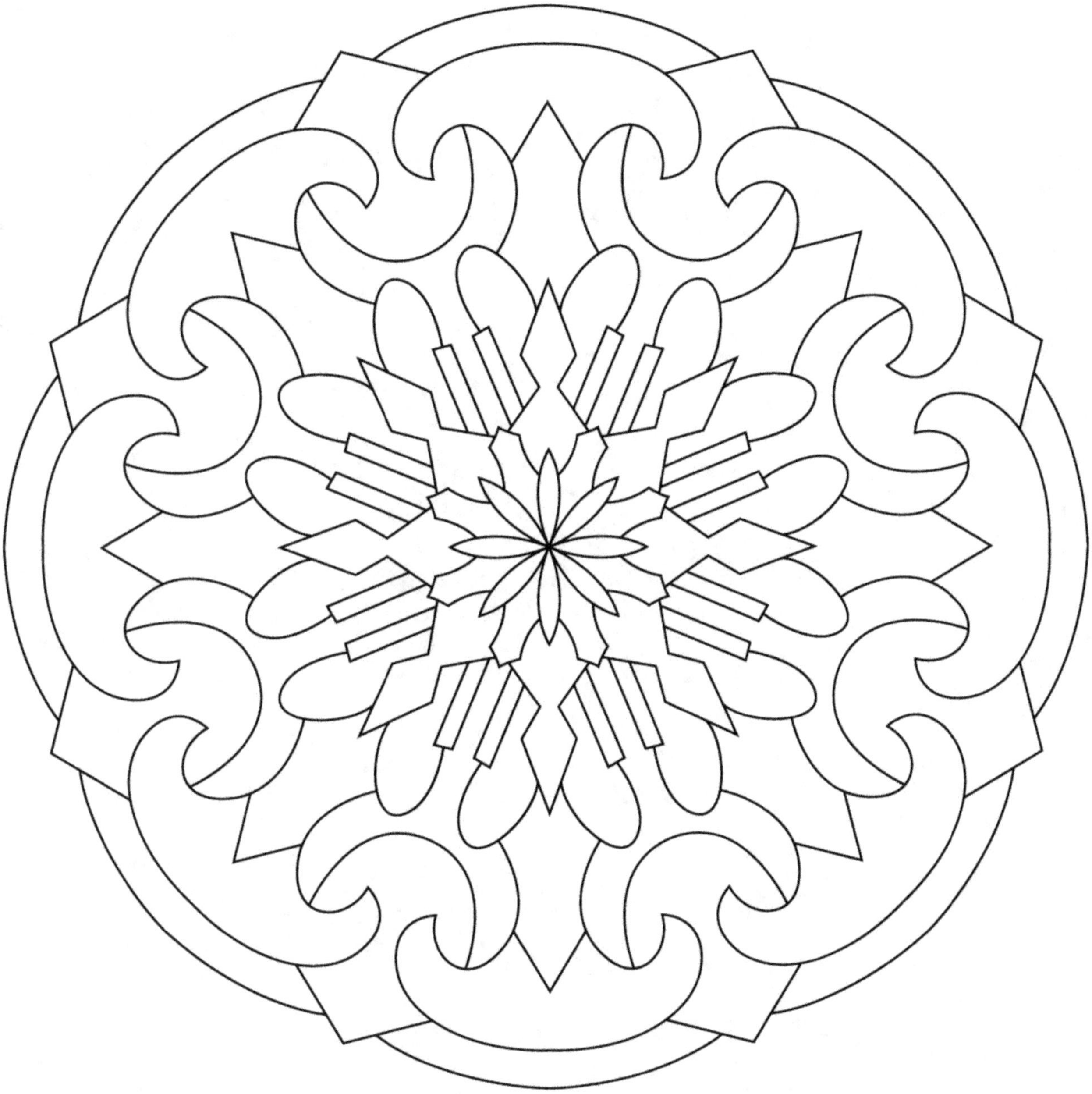

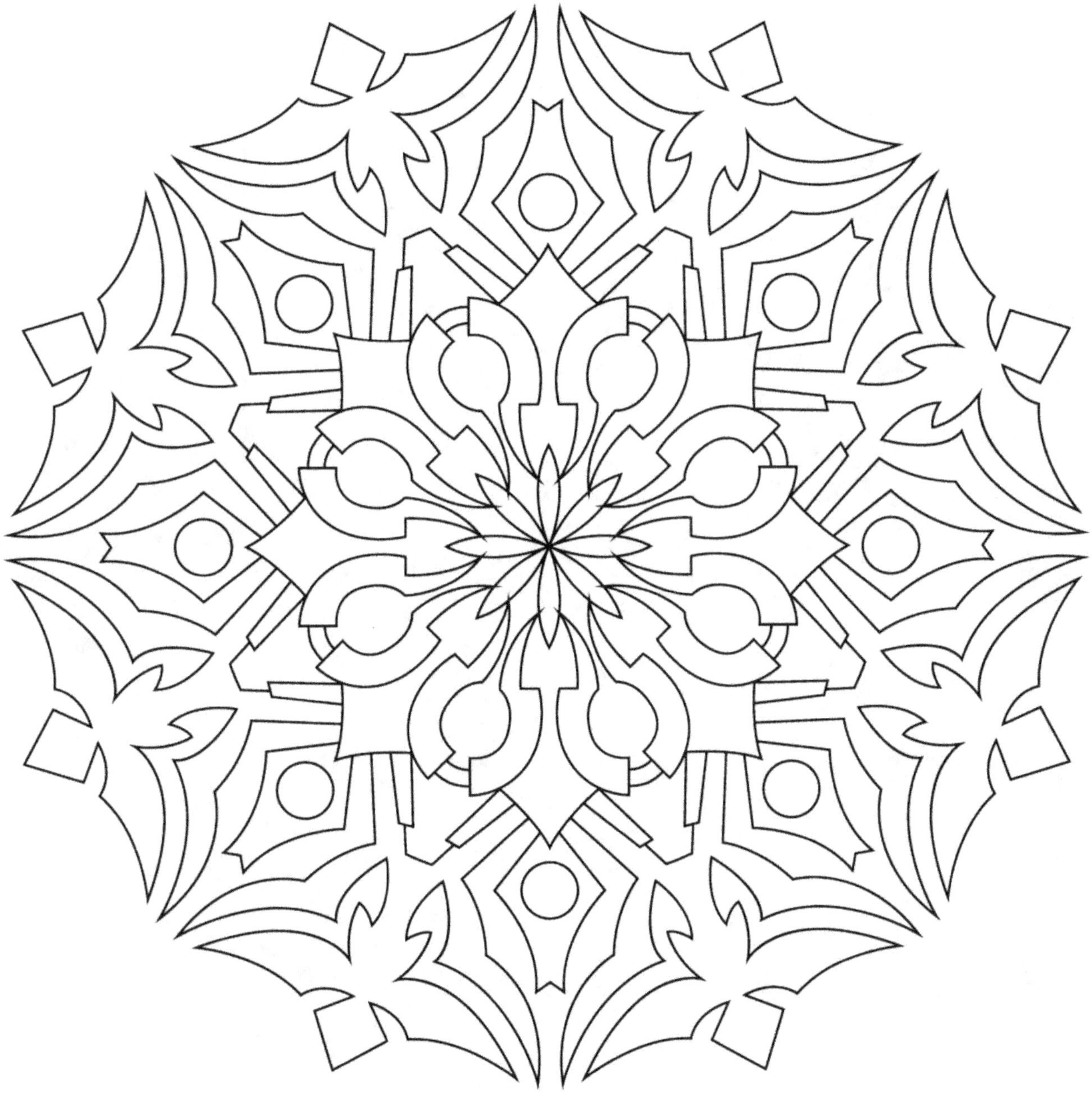

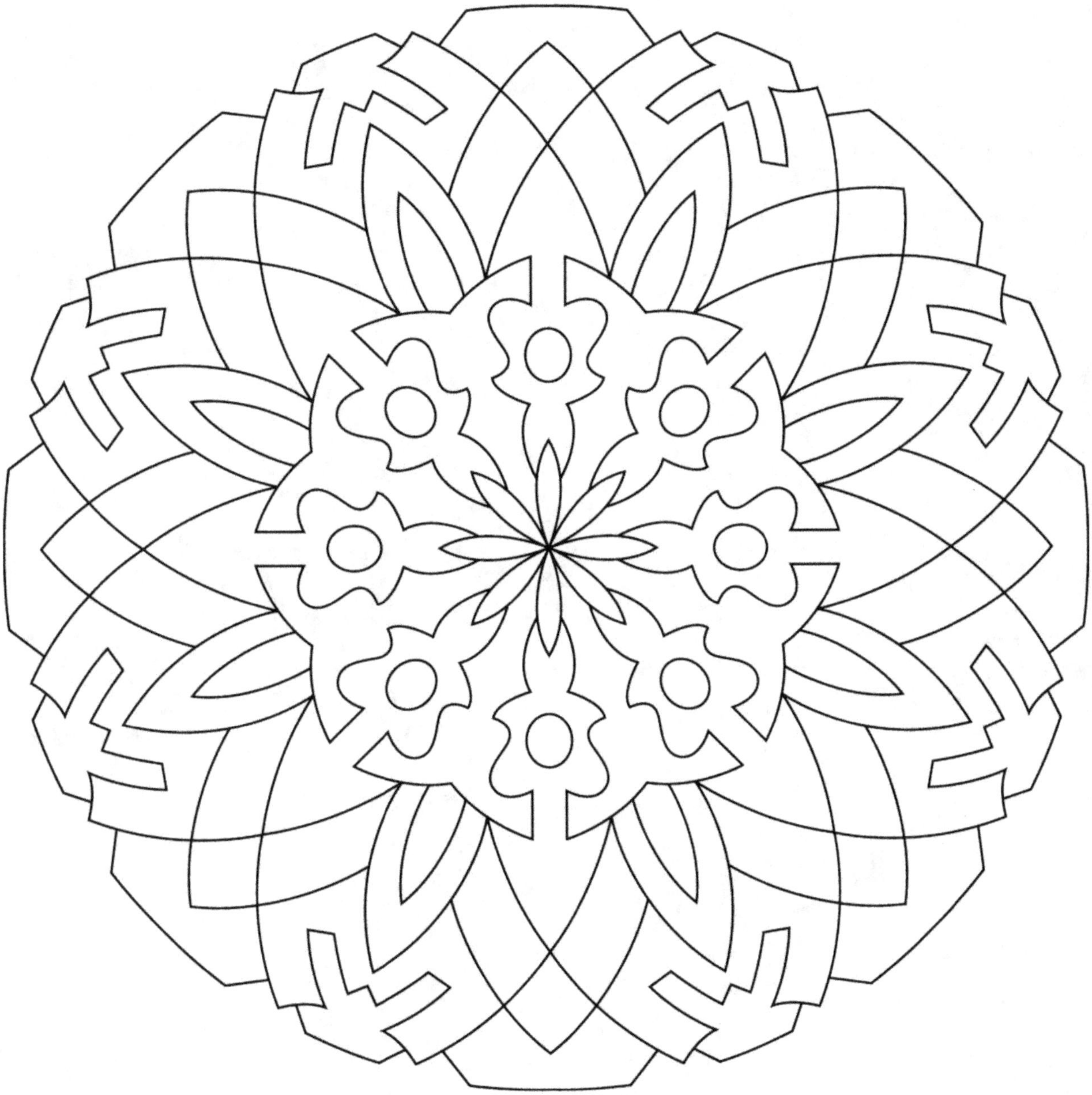

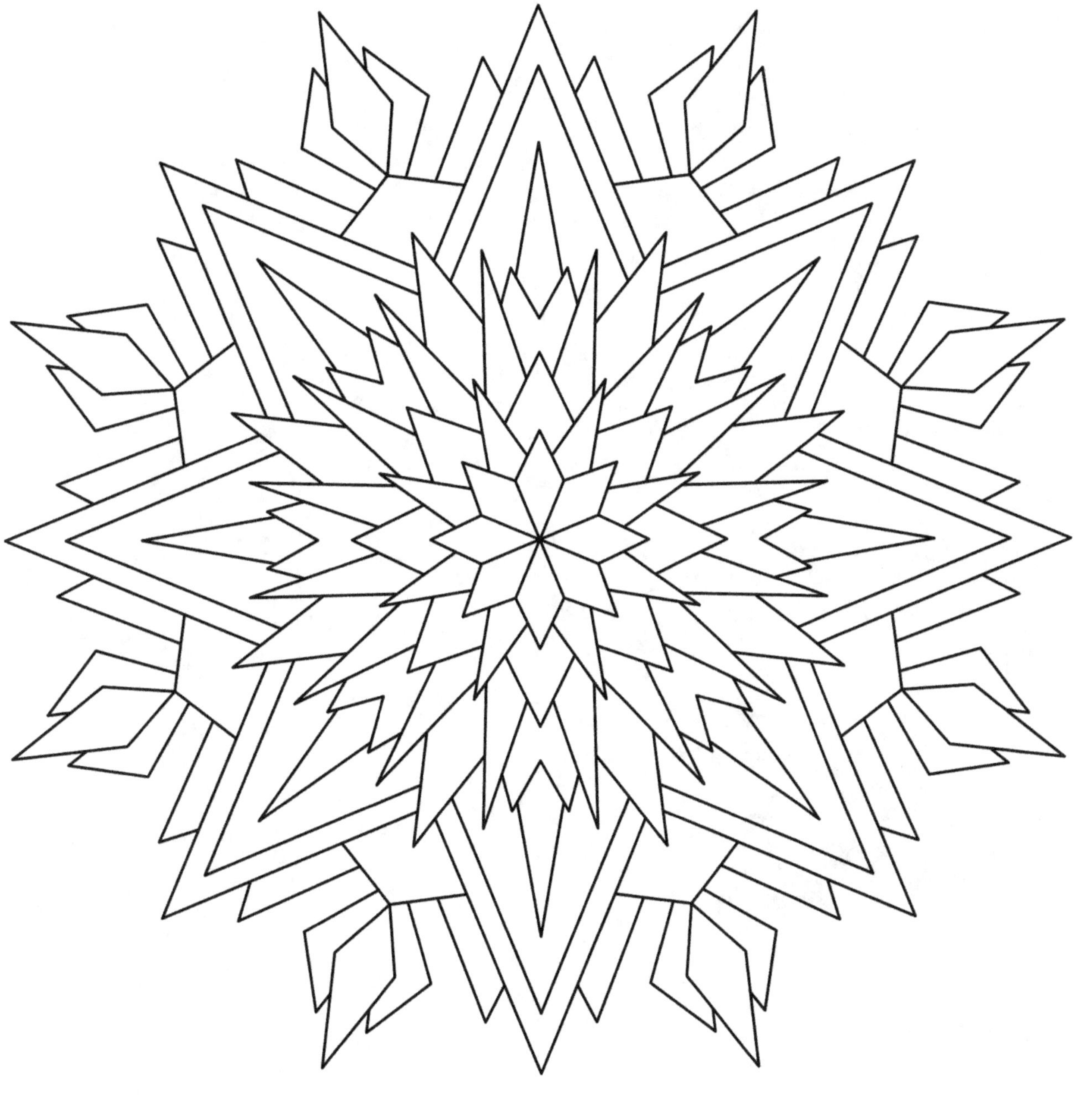

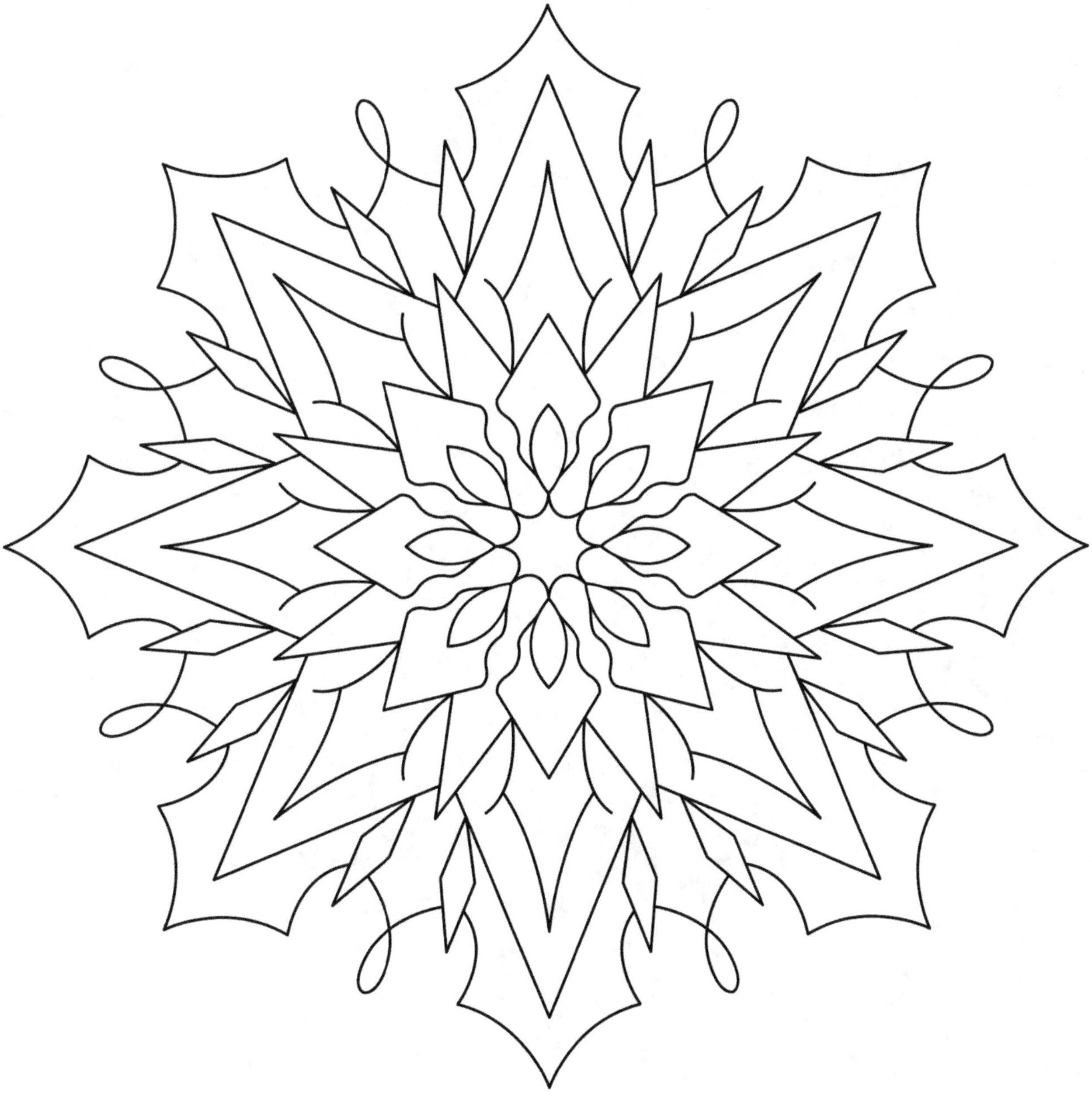

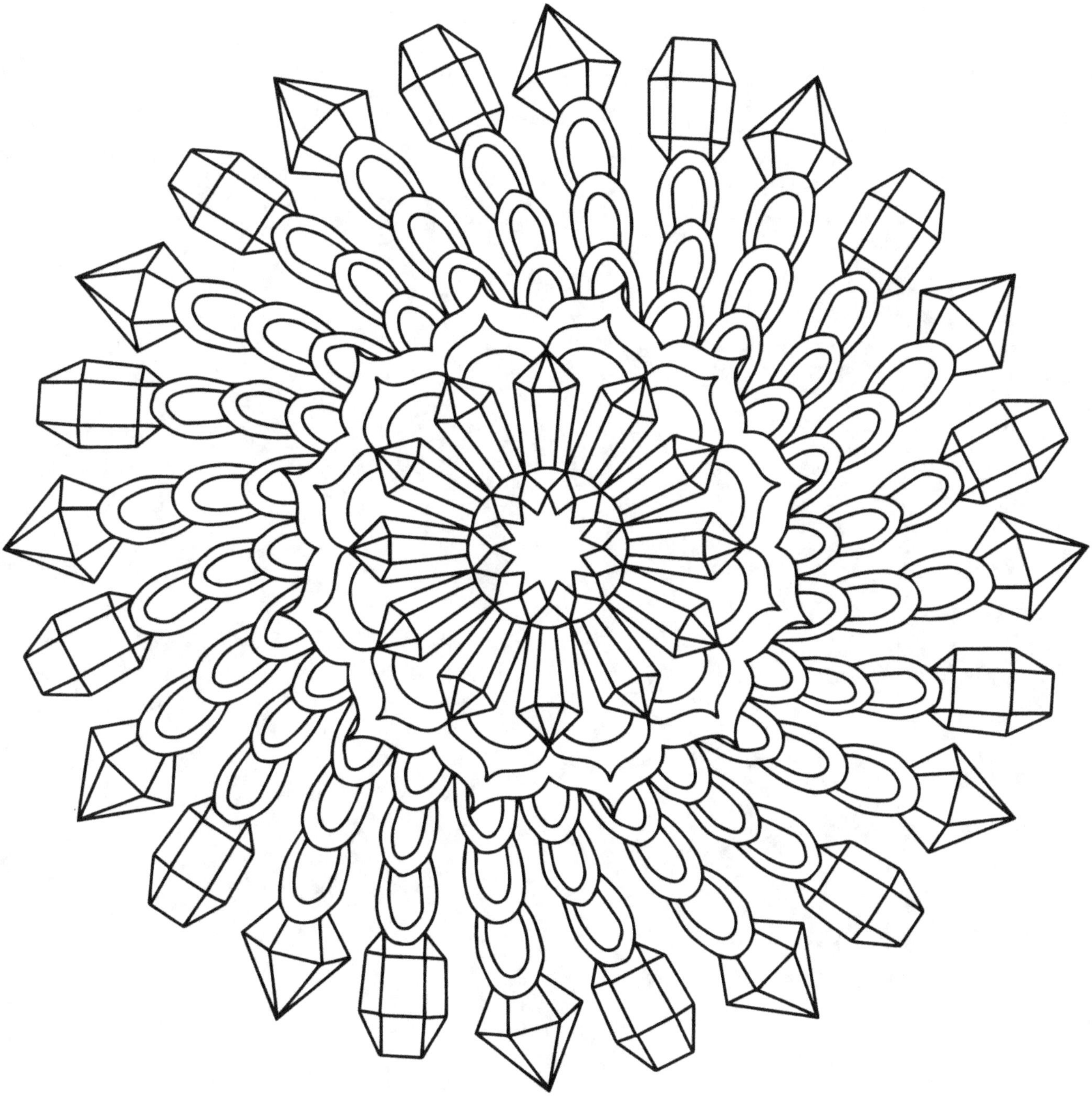

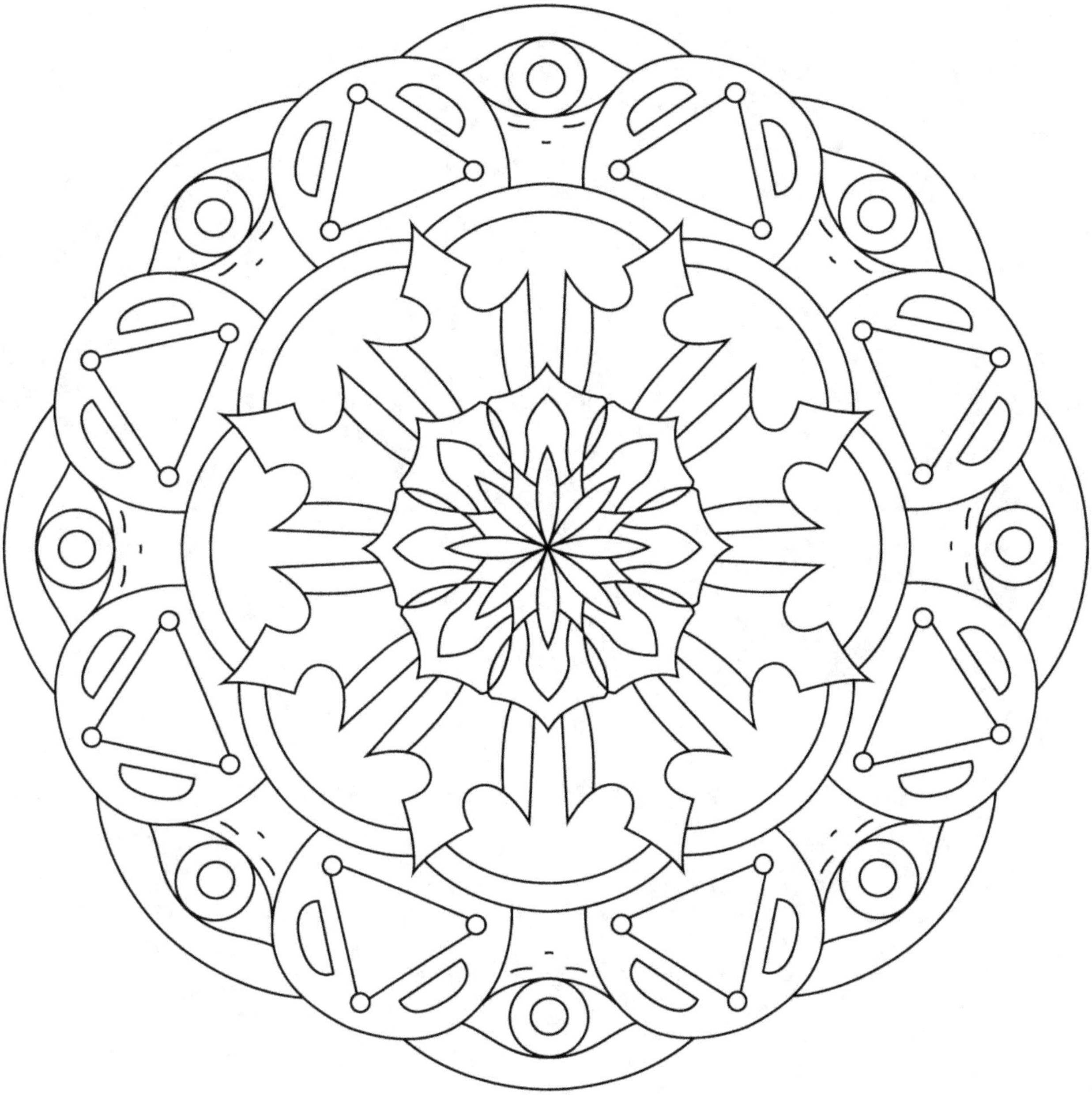

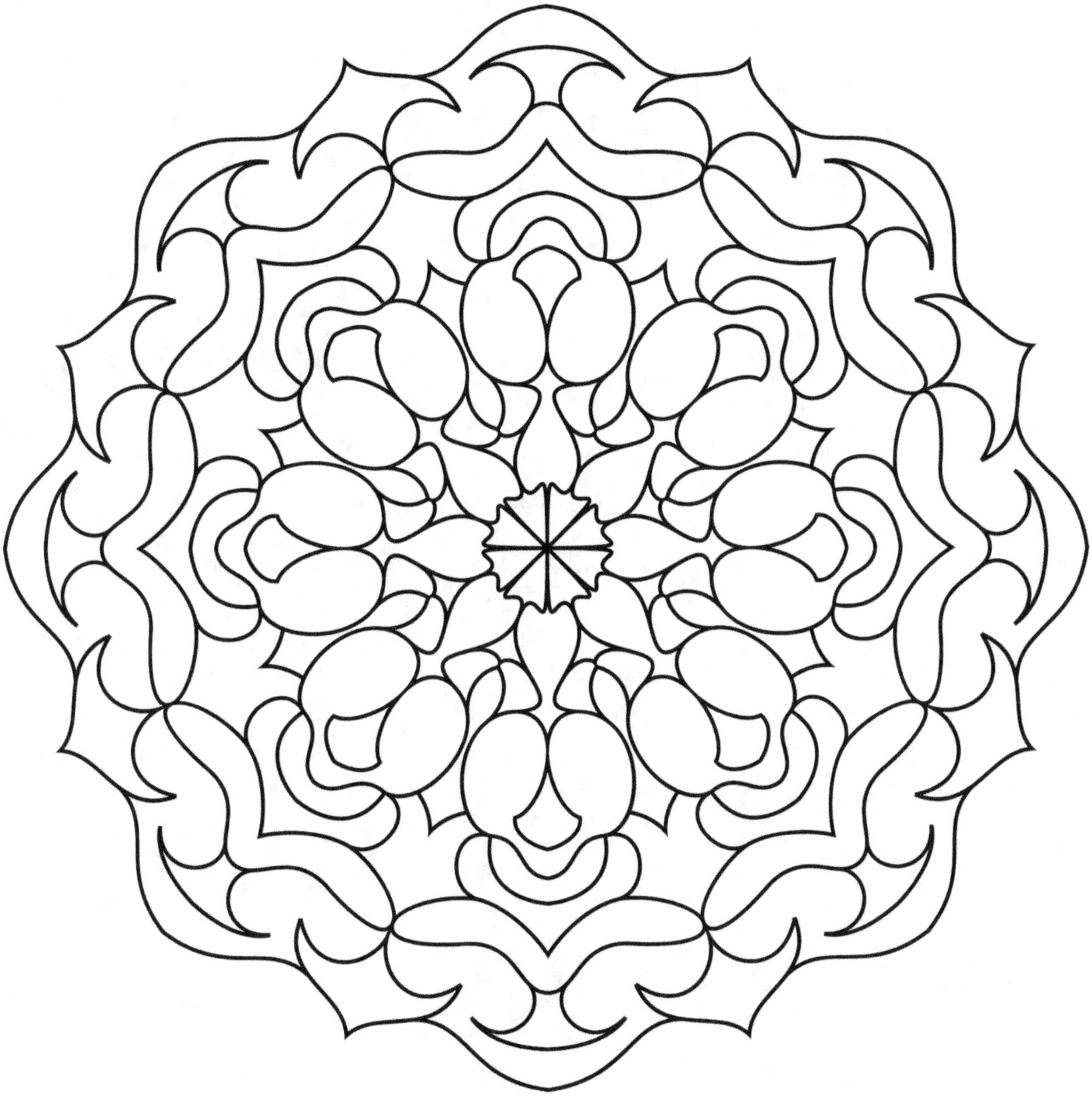

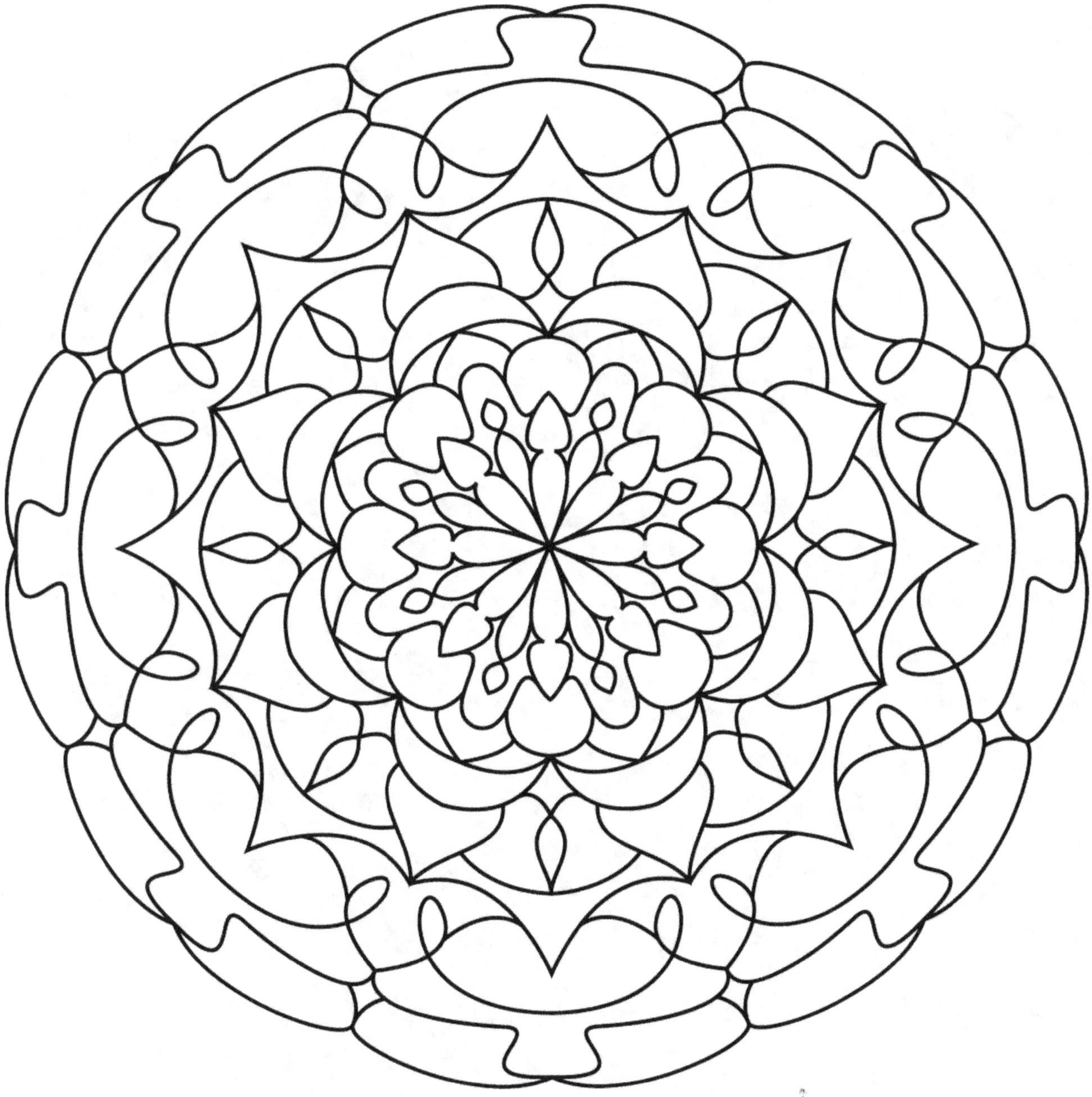

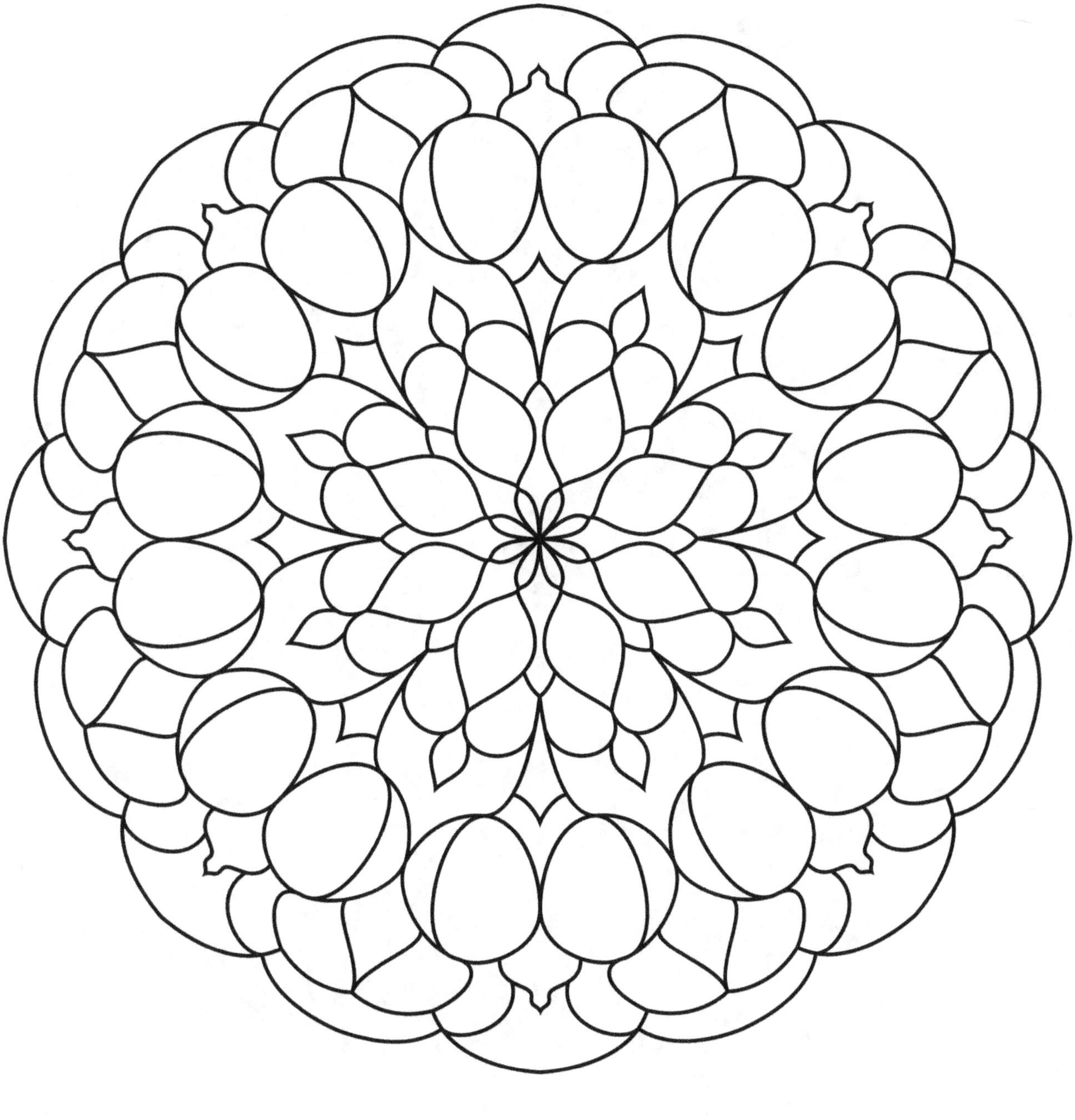

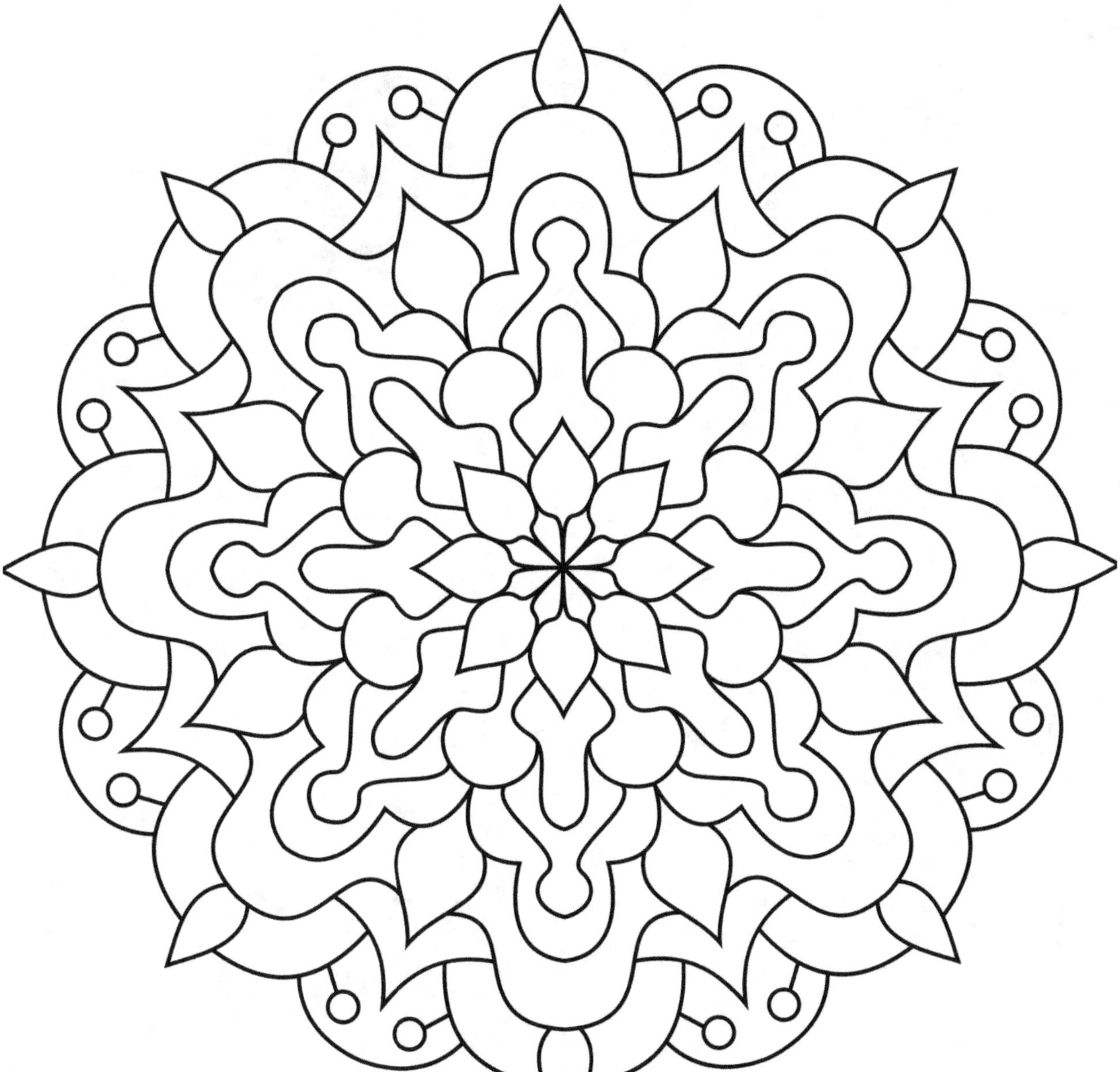

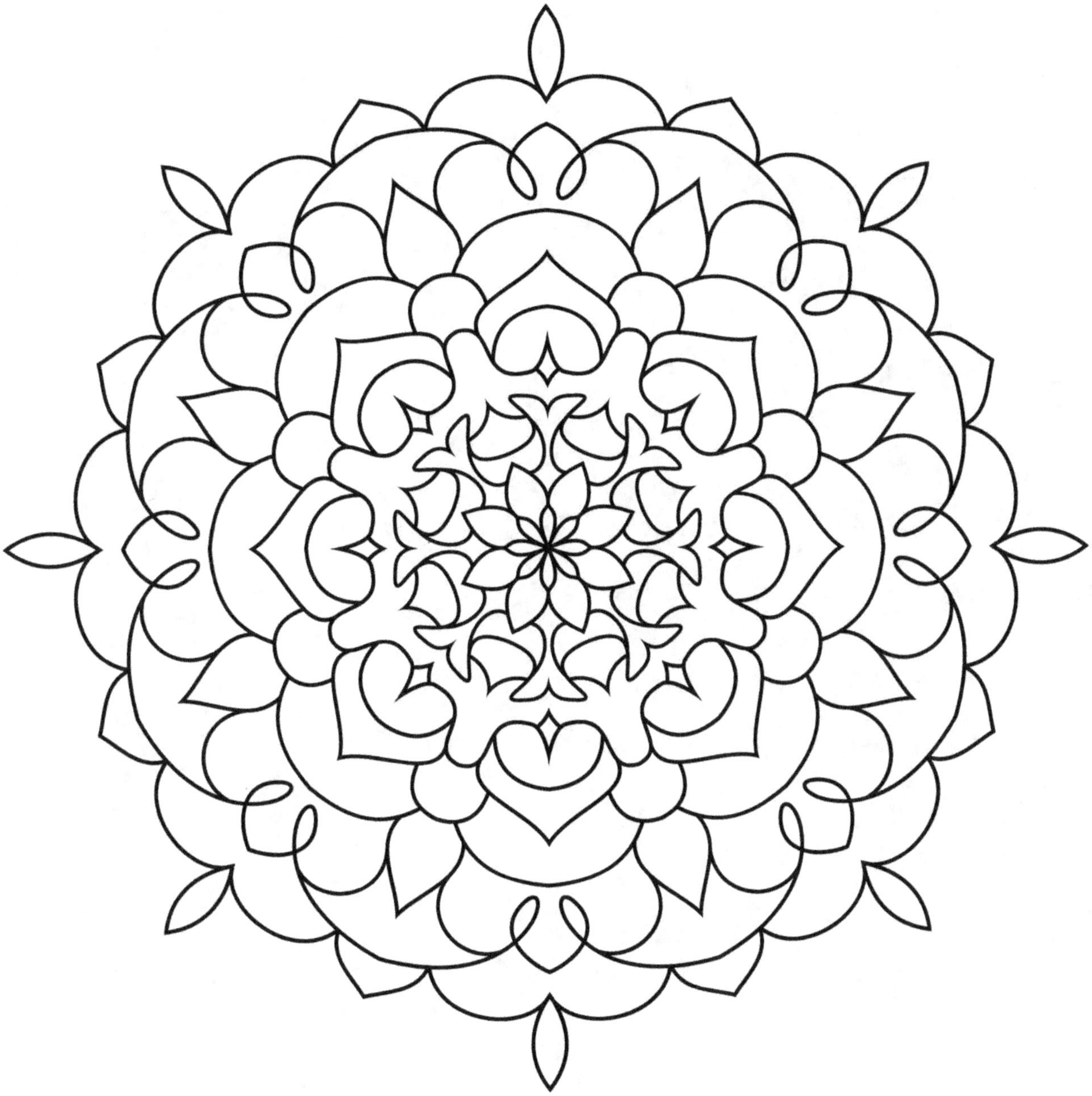

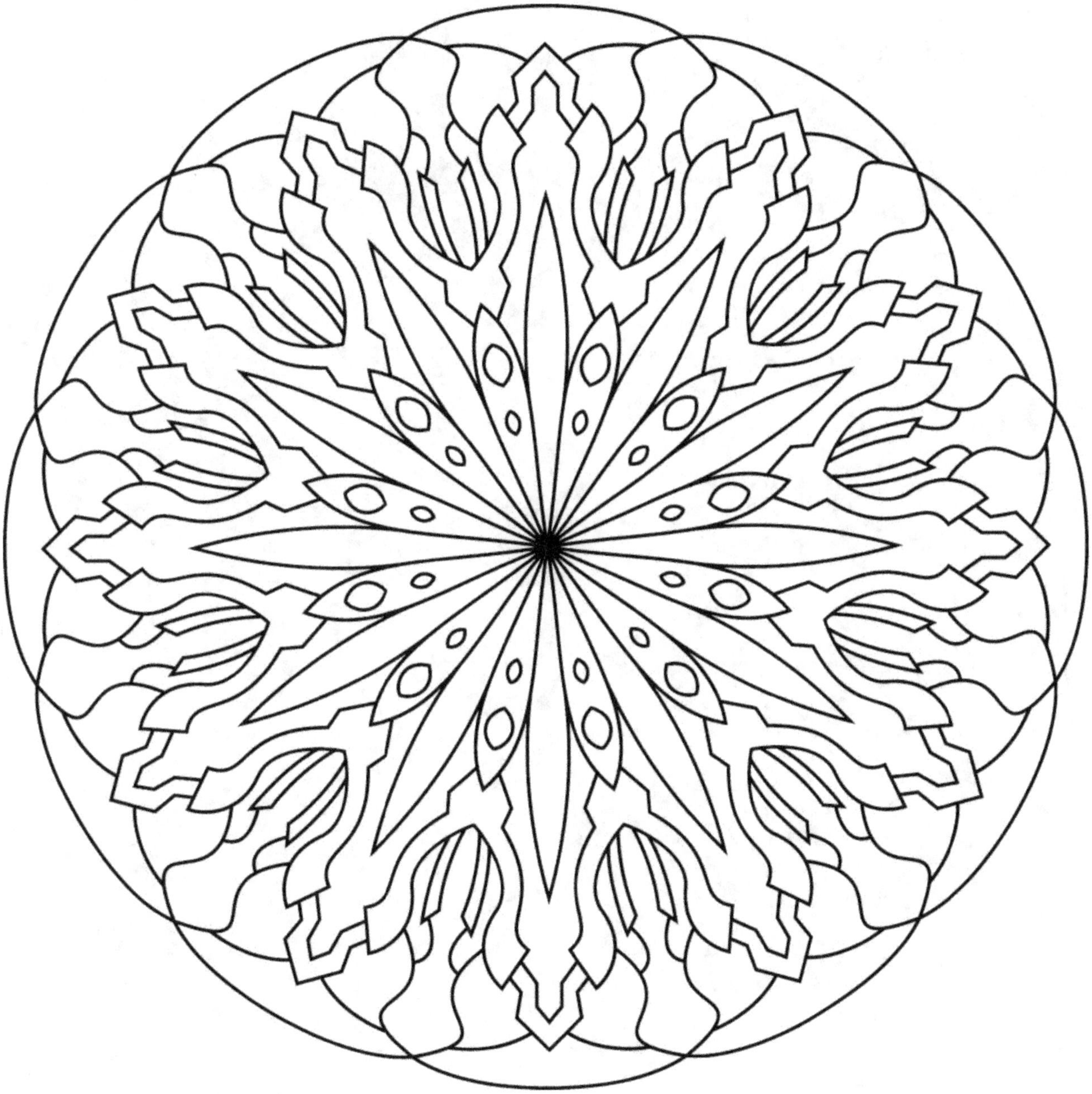

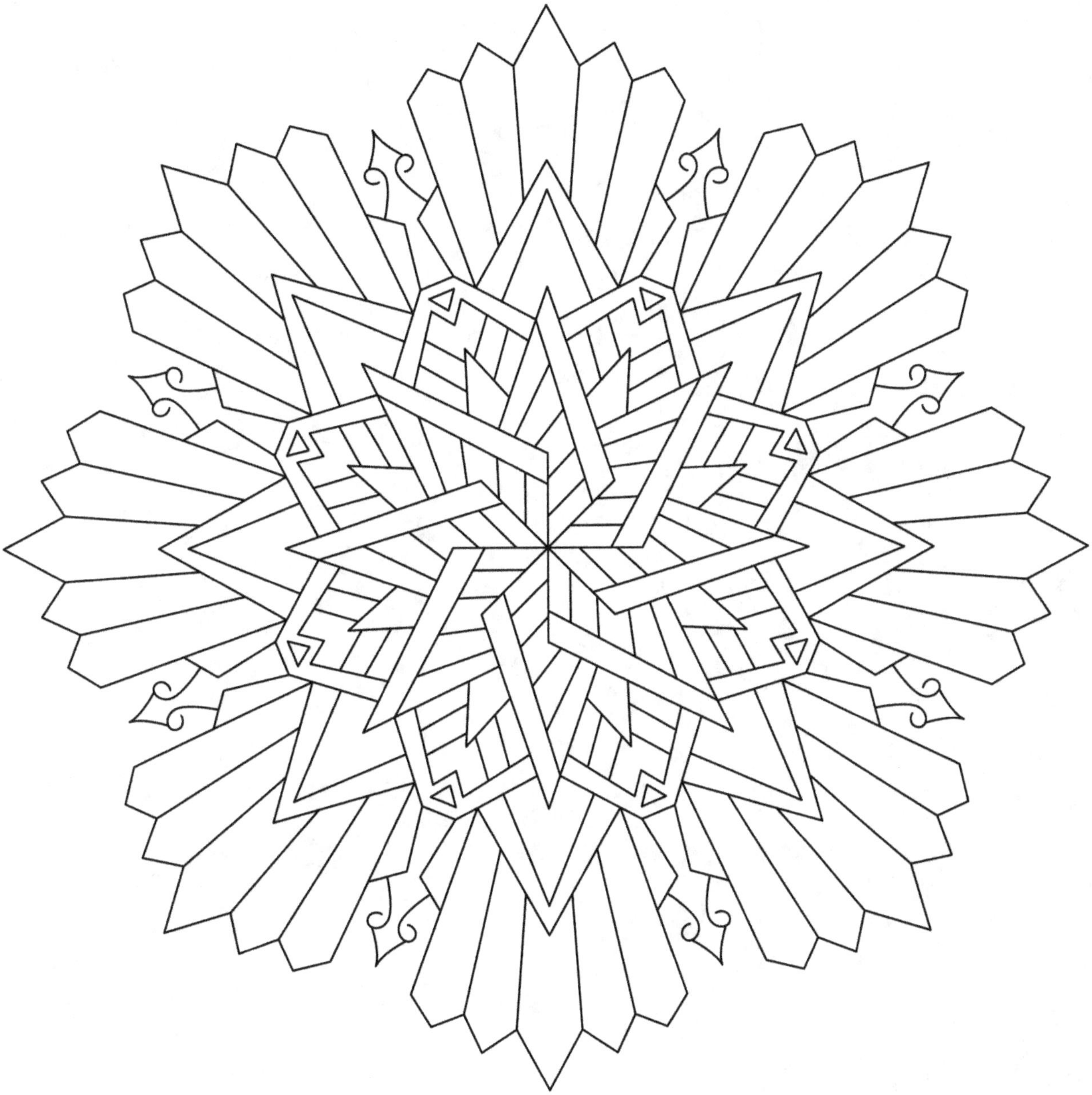

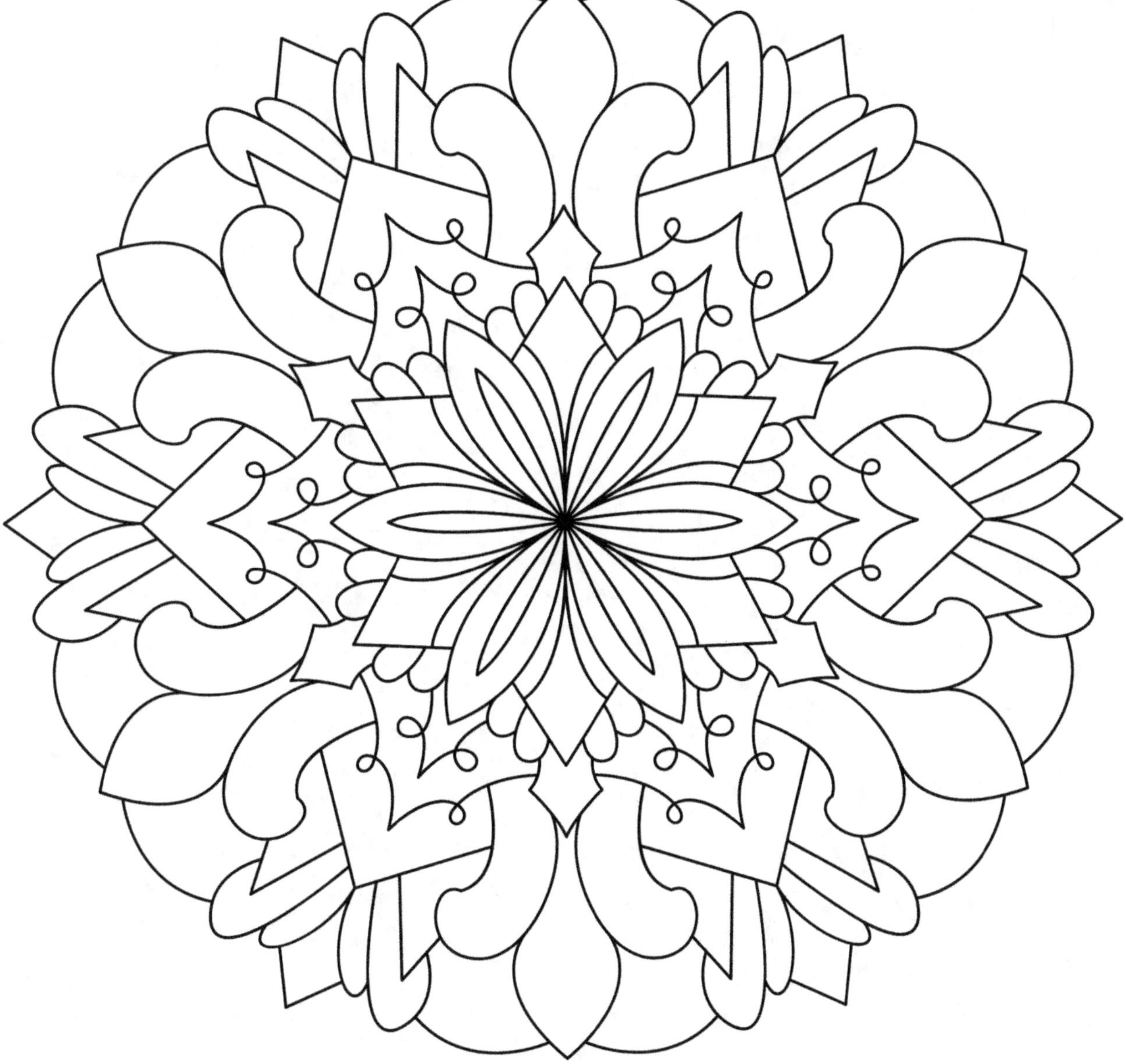

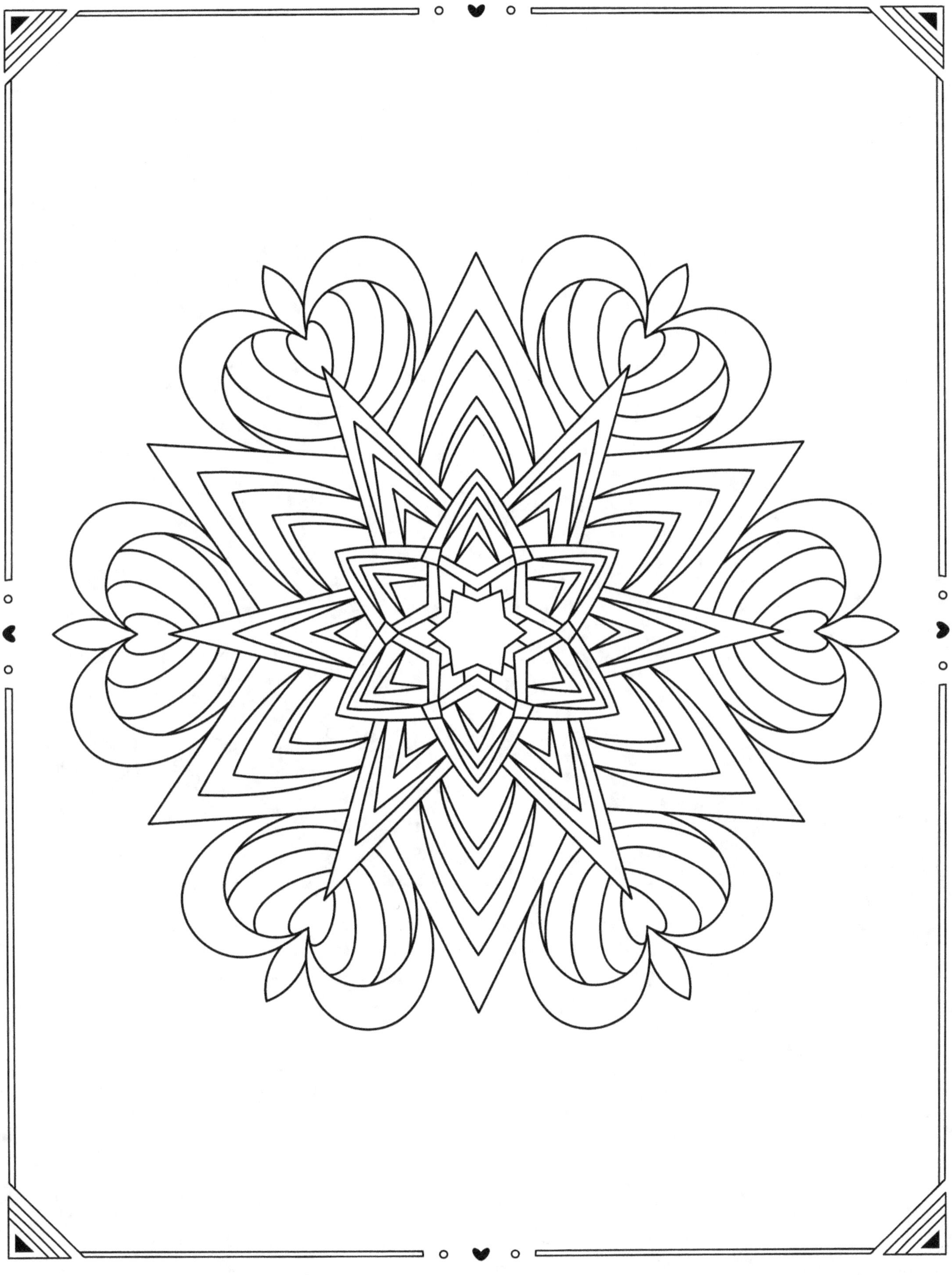

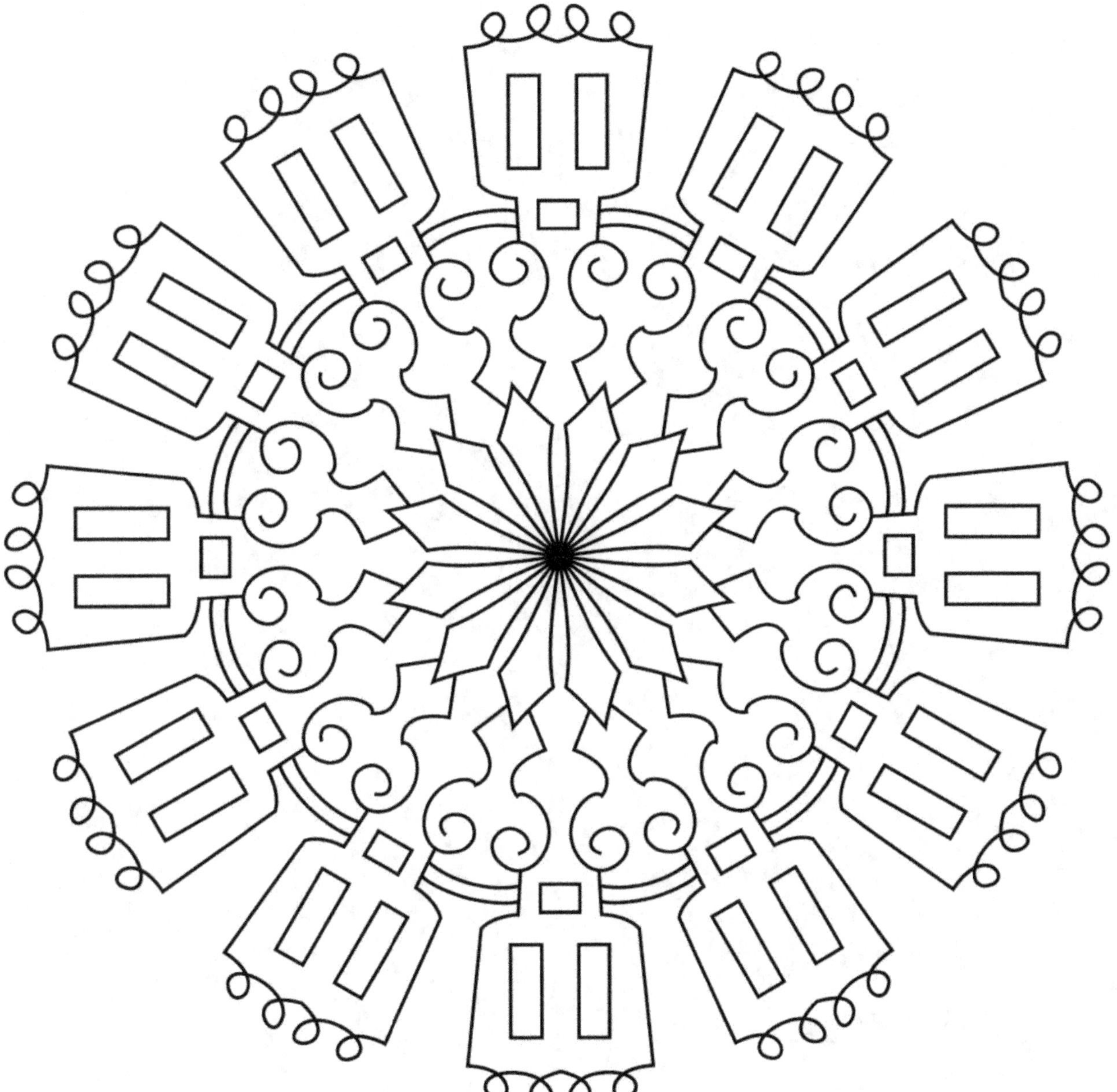

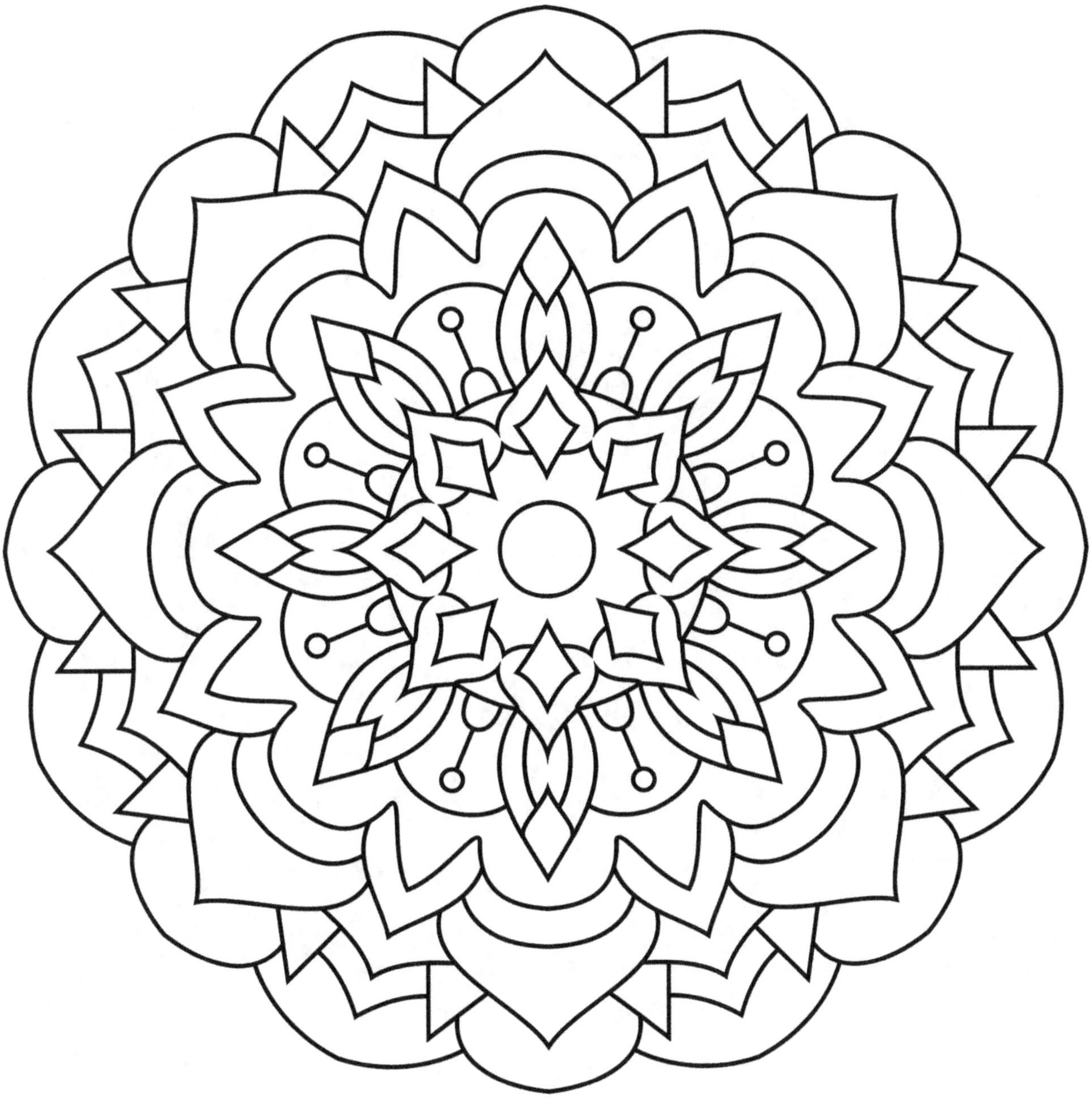

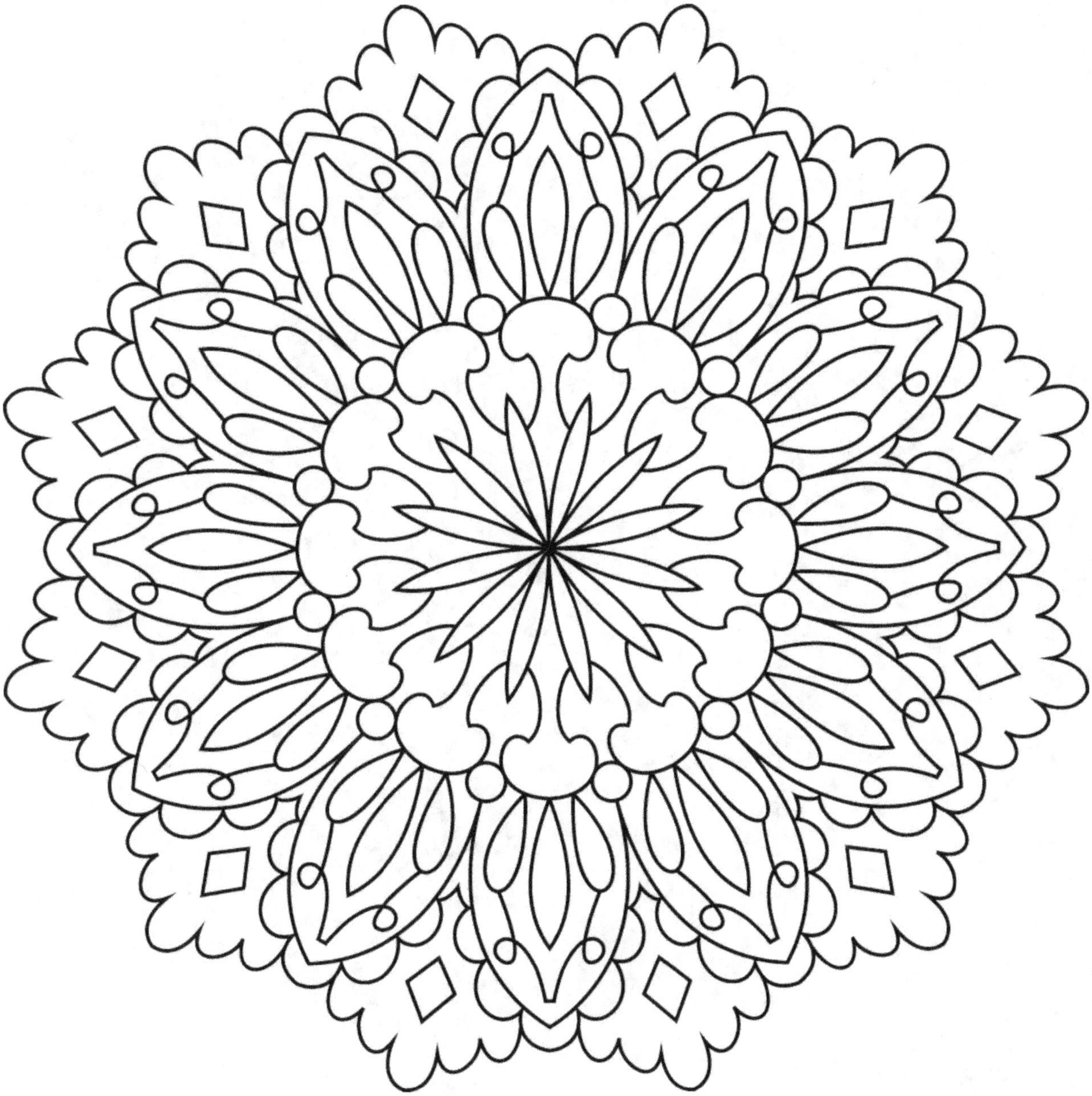

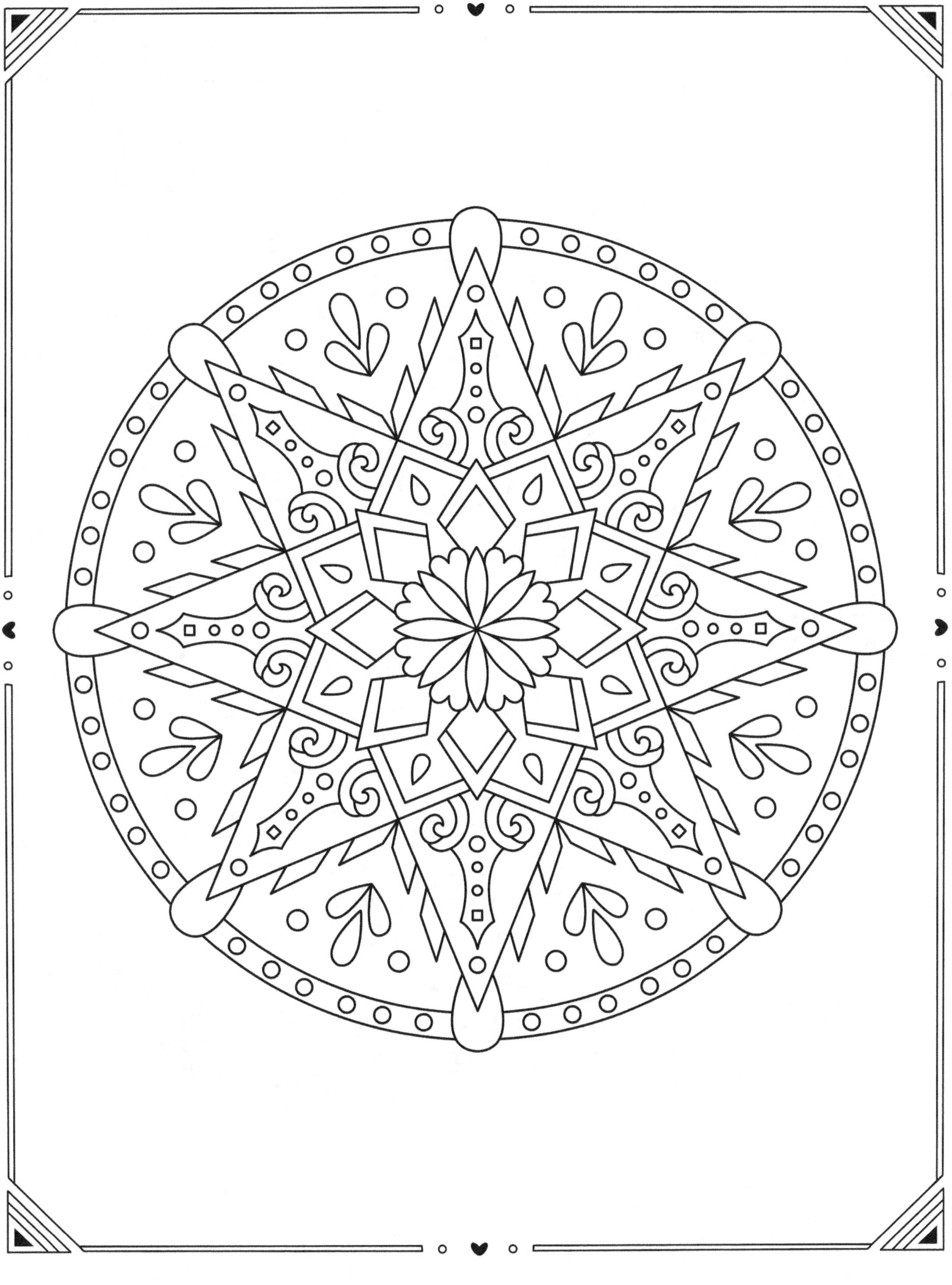

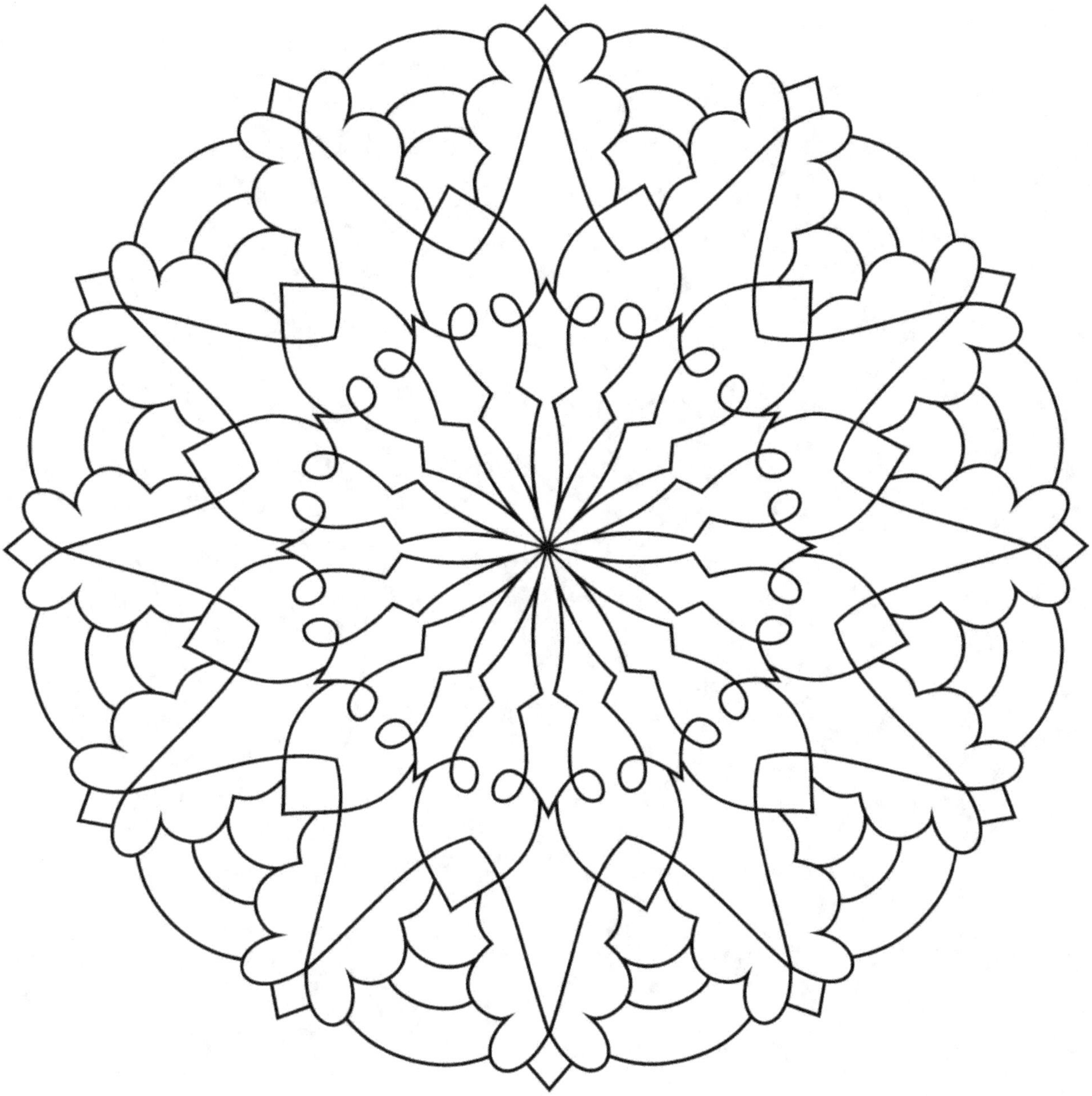

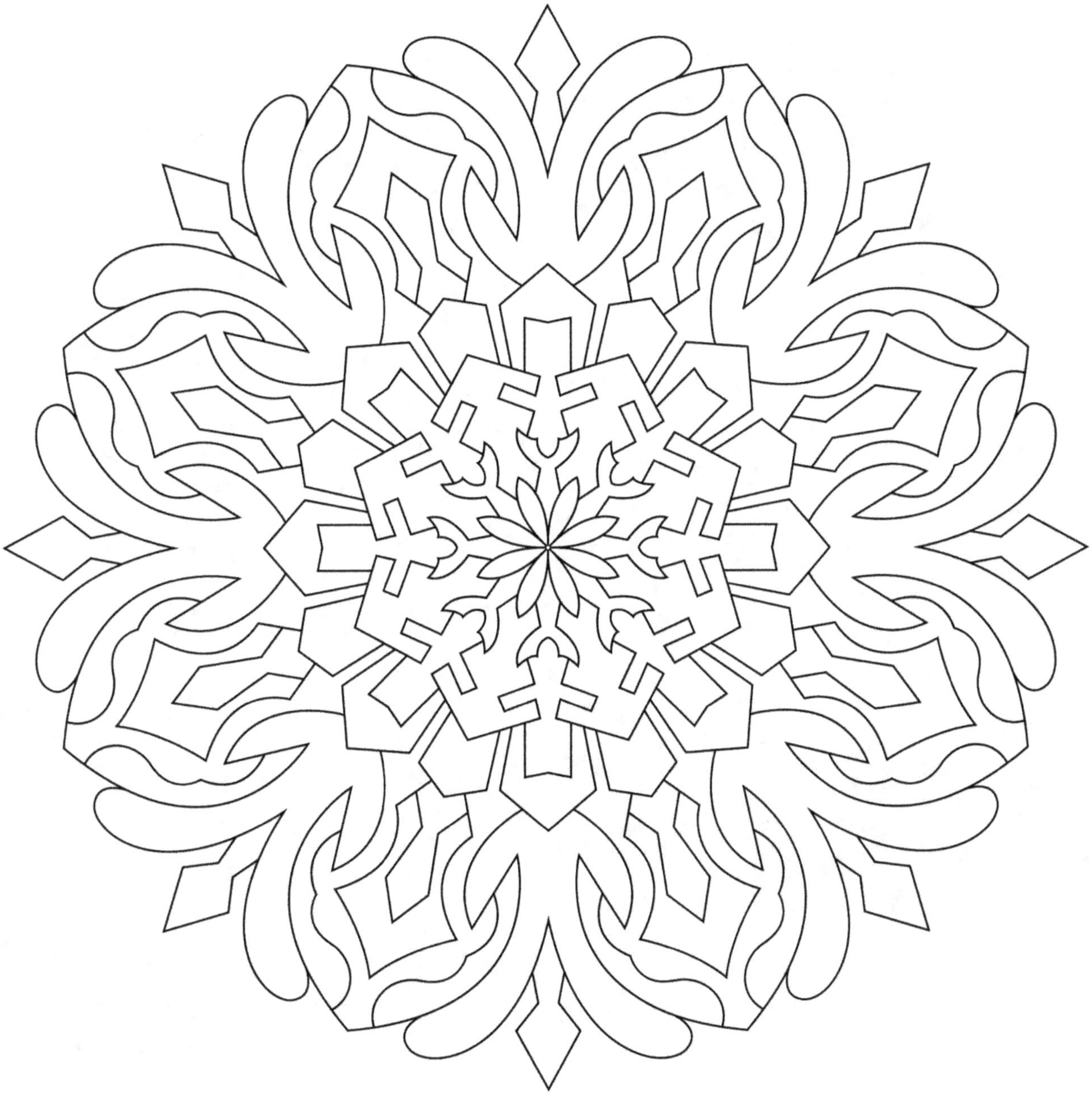

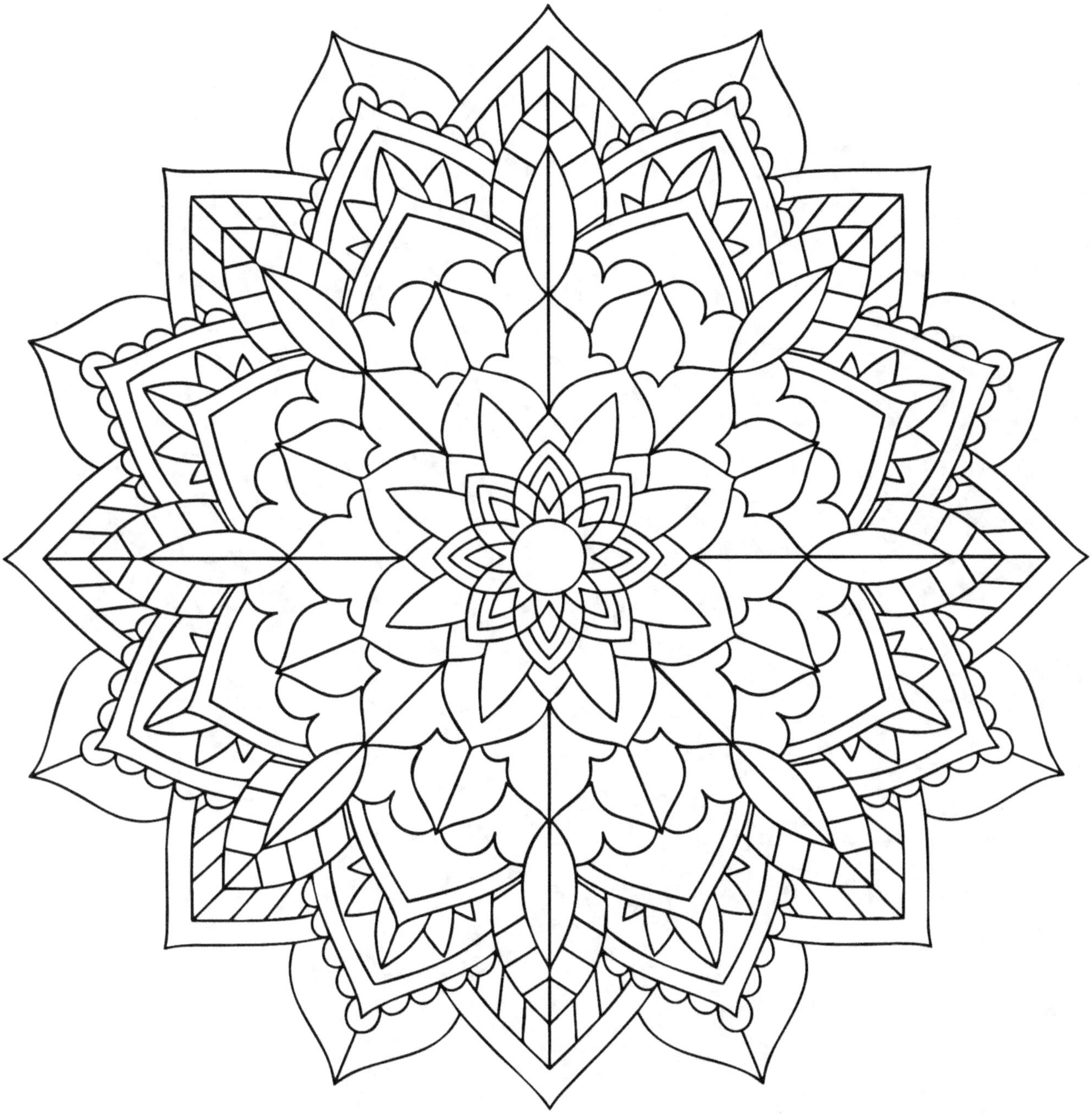

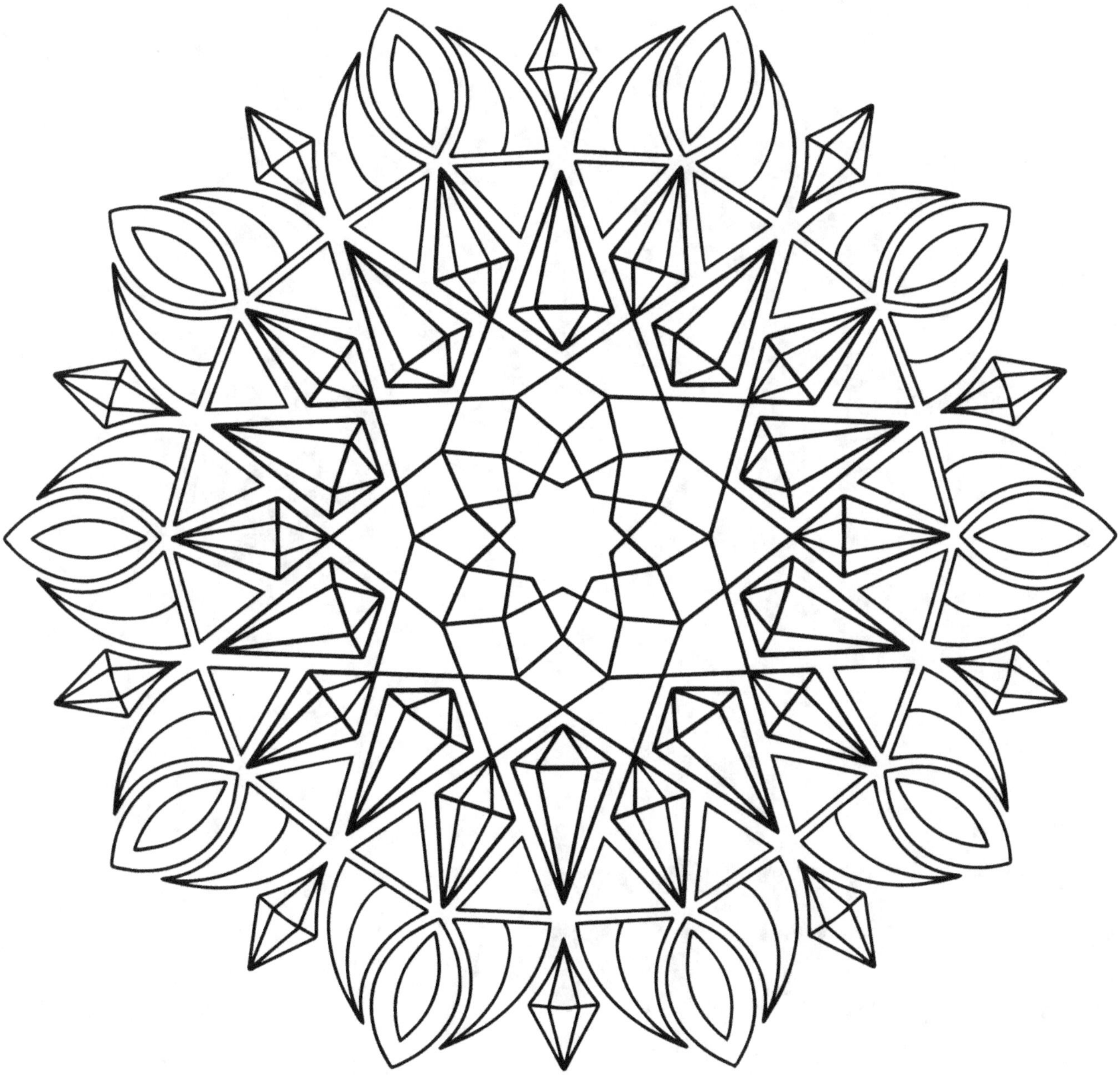

www.ingramcontent.com/pod-product-compliance
Lightning Source LLC
Chambersburg PA
CBHW080505220526
45465CB00006B/2382
* 9 7 9 8 3 5 6 8 4 8 8 8 9 *